GREAT LIVES OBSERVED

Gerald Emanuel Stearn, *General Editor*

EACH VOLUME IN THE SERIES VIEWS THE CHARACTER AND ACHIEVE-
MENT OF A GREAT WORLD FIGURE IN THREE PERSPECTIVES—
THROUGH HIS OWN WORDS, THROUGH THE OPINIONS OF HIS CON-
TEMPORARIES, AND THROUGH RETROSPECTIVE JUDGMENTS—THUS
COMBINING THE INTIMACY OF AUTOBIOGRAPHY, THE IMMEDIACY
OF EYEWITNESS OBSERVATION, AND THE OBJECTIVITY OF MODERN
SCHOLARSHIP.

EMMA LOU THORNBROUGH, *the editor of this volume in the
Great Lives Observed series, is Professor of History at Butler
University. Her most recently published books include* Since
Emancipation: A Short History of Indiana Negroes, 1863–
1963 *and* Indiana in the Civil War Era, 1850–1880.

Forthcoming volumes in the Great Lives Observed series:

Cromwell, edited by Maurice Ashley

John F. Kennedy, edited by Barton J. Bernstein

Huey Long, edited by Hugh Davis Graham

Mao, edited by Jerome Ch'en

Joseph McCarthy, edited by Allen Matusow

Woodrow Wilson, edited by John Braeman

GREAT LIVES OBSERVED

Booker T.
Washington

Edited by
EMMA LOU THORNBROUGH

A SPECTRUM BOOK

PRENTICE-HALL, INC., ENGLEWOOD CLIFFS, N.J.

Contents

v

PART TWO

BOOKER T. WASHINGTON VIEWED BY HIS CONTEMPORARIES

PART THREE

BOOKER T. WASHINGTON IN HISTORY

Introduction

To understand a man it is necessary to know something of the times in which he lived. Booker T. Washington was born in 1856 and died in 1915. His lifetime spanned the period from the Civil War to the First World War. It was an era of unparalleled material growth and change during which the United States emerged as the leading industrial nation in the world. It was the age of "big business," in which men like Rockefeller and Carnegie were free to exercise their entrepreneurial and acquisitive talents without interference from government. It was the age of Social Darwinism, which defended unfettered competition as indispensable to economic progress. It was the age of the Gospel of Wealth, which preached the God-given right of men of ability to amass as much wealth as they could but also stressed their obligation to give to philanthropic enterprises. It was the age of the Horatio Alger novels, which told the story of poor boys who made good and reiterated the moral that opportunities for success—considered synonymous with material gain—were available to all who were virtuous and hardworking.

However, the Horatio Alger heroes were always white boys; for the mass of Negro Americans the age of Booker T. Washington coincided with the period which one historian has called the "nadir." [1] Washington reached his twenty-first birthday in 1877—the year which marked the overthrow of the last of the Reconstruction governments in which Negroes had played a meaningful part. The Compromise of 1877 by which President Hayes and his northern Republican supporters established a modus vivendi with the white redeemer governments of the former Confederate States meant the end of efforts by the federal government to protect southern Negroes in the exercise of their political rights.

The abandonment of federal intervention in the South reflected a growing disillusionment in the North over the fruits of Reconstruction and the conviction that the South should be free to solve its problems without outside interference. There followed a great re-

[1] Rayford W. Logan, *The Negro in American Life and Thought: The Nadir, 1877–1901* (New York, 1954).

1

conciliation between white northerners and white southerners, but this sectional rapprochement was at the expense of southern Negroes. By the 1890's, when Washington emerged as a national figure, bitterness resulting from the Civil War and Reconstruction had largely dissipated. To a remarkable degree dominant groups in the two sections appeared to share the same views on matters pertaining to race.

With few exceptions white Americans assumed that Negroes were inherently inferior. This assumption was constantly reinforced by a voluminous literature—both scholarly and popular—by newspapers, by political speeches, and by sermons. Scientists concerned with problems of evolution and genetics assumed or claimed to demonstrate the existence of innate racial differences and capacities. Both scientists and social scientists warned of the deleterious effects of racial mixing. Even so distinguished and humanitarian a sociologist as Lester Ward asserted that Negro men raped white women because of the "biological imperative" of improving their offspring and that the same reason impelled Negro women to submit to white men. Similar ideas were expressed in more sensational form in books with such titles as *The Negro, A Menace to American Civilization* and *The Negro A Beast,* and in the novels of Thomas Dixon. Newspapers were full of stories of Negro atrocities and cartoons depicting Negroes as bestial.[2]

Historians, like scientists, were consciously or unconsciously racists. They subscribed to the doctrine of the superiority of the "Teutonic race." By the turn of the century historians, like northerners generally, were convinced that Radical Reconstruction had been a tragic mistake. Some northerners agreed with southerners that Negroes had retrogressed since Emancipation. More of them admitted that they thought that the granting of political rights to Negroes had been premature. Even those who had been abolitionists and champions of Negro rights were ready to acquiesce in disfranchisement. In a significant editorial in the *Nation* in 1890, E. L. Godkin commented on the "rapidly growing sympathy at the North with southern perplexity over the negro problem." He expressed the view that bestowing suffrage had been a mistake and opposed any more "sacrifices" for the benefit of Negroes, including the adoption of the Lodge Federal Elections Bill then pending in Congress.[3]

[2] A good summary of racial thought in the period is I. A. Newby, *Jim Crow's Defense: Anti-Negro Thought in America, 1900–1930* (Baton Rouge, 1965).
[3] "The Negro Problem," *The Nation,* L (January 23, 1890), 64.

Meanwhile decisions of the United States Supreme Court gave further evidence of the abandonment of the southern Negro by the federal government. In the Civil Rights Cases of 1883 the Court, with only one dissenting vote, had declared unconstitutional the portion of the Civil Rights Act of 1875 in which Congress had prohibited racial discrimination in the use of public accommodations. In 1896, in *Plessy v. Ferguson,* the Court held that a Louisiana statute requiring segregation of whites and Negroes in railroad coaches did not violate the Fourteenth Amendment. In 1898 the Court upheld the suffrage section of the Mississippi Constitution which was designed to disfranchise Negroes by means of an "understanding" test for voting. Thereafter state after state followed the example of Mississippi; by 1910 Negroes had been virtually eliminated as voters in all southern and border states.

Disfranchisement was accompanied by the adoption of more and more stringent Jim Crow laws. There was a proliferation of state and local segregation laws, ranging from residential zoning ordinances and separate coach laws to ordinances which prohibited white and Negro laborers from working in the same room of a factory.

The white supremacists, who were firmly in control of southern politics, argued that segregation and the elimination of Negroes from participation in politics would improve race relations by removing causes of friction. But the reverse occurred. Lynchings of Negroes in the United States reached a peak in the period between 1890 and 1910. Race riots occurred in several southern cities in the wake of disfranchisement campaigns. Distinguished whites like the historian John Spencer Bassett and Negroes like the novelist Charles W. Chesnutt agreed that race prejudice was more intense in the early years of the twentieth century than at any previous time and that the position of the Negro had deteriorated.[4]

The child who was later to be known as Booker T. Washington was born on April 5, 1856. His birth and the conditions of his early years were typical of the slave system. His mother, Jane, was a slave and the cook on a small plantation in the back country of Virginia. His father was a white man, but except that he came from a neighboring plantation, the child knew nothing of his identity. In fact he was never even sure of the year of his own birth. His mother called him

[4] A good summary is C. Vann Woodward, *The Strange Career of Jim Crow: A Brief Account of Segregation* (New York, 1955).

Booker, but he had no last name until he went to school. When he realized that all of the other children at school had a "second" name and the teacher asked him his, he invented the name Washington, and henceforth he and his brothers (John, who was also the son of a white man, and James, who was adopted) used the name.

In his autobiography, *Up From Slavery,* which gives an unforgettable picture of his childhood, Washington said that as a boy he tried to imagine what it would have been like to be a white boy with an honored family name and distinguished ancestry. He remarked that white people who constantly called attention to the "moral weaknesses" of Negro youths and compared them unfavorably with white youths did "not consider the influence of the memories which cling about the old family homesteads." A proud family history and the desire to perpetuate it gave white boys a stimulus to succeed which Negroes lacked. On the other hand, Washington said, if he had been "a member of a more popular race," he might have been inclined to rely upon his ancestry and color to do for him what he should have done for himself.

Certainly, even as a boy, he did not allow the circumstances of his birth to deter him from moving "up from slavery." In fact, the entire story of his life became an impressive example of the American success story—a story of remarkable achievements in the face of almost insurmountable obstacles.

After the Civil War ended, Jane and her children moved to Malden, West Virginia, where Washington Ferguson, a former slave to whom she was now married, had found employment in the salt mines. At the age of nine Booker also went to work in the mines. But in spite of gruelling labor he managed to enroll for a time in a local school for Negroes. In 1871 he left the mines to go to work as a houseboy in the home of General Lewis Ruffin, owner of the mines. His association with Mrs. Ruffin, a strict New Englander, was to be one of the important influences in his life. From her he learned respect for cleanliness and pride in a job well done.

At sixteen the boy took what was probably the most decisive step in his life when he resolved to enter Hampton Institute in Virginia. Hampton, which had opened in 1868, was the product of the inspiration and effort of General Samuel C. Armstrong, the son of American missionaries in Hawaii. Armstrong was convinced that the ultimate solution of the problems of the Negro freedmen lay in education— but education of a practical and utilitarian nature which would teach the skills necessary for earning a livelihood and at the same time develop character and morality.

Young Washington, who traveled most of the distance from Malden by foot, arrived at Hampton penniless and dirty. Nevertheless, he was able to persuade the authorities to admit him and to give him a janitorial job which helped to pay his expenses. As a student he received instruction in basic academic subjects and also learned practical lessons in agriculture. He also learned some even more basic lessons in personal cleanliness and conduct, and by participating in the debating society, he began to develop his talent for public speaking. But the most important part of his experience at Hampton was the association with General Armstrong, whom Washington described in his autobiography as "a great man—the noblest, rarest human being that it has ever been my privilege to meet." Not only did Armstrong become Washington's model as an educator; in later years he also helped his pupil gain access to the northern philanthropists who played an indispensable role in the development of Tuskegee.

For three years after graduation from Hampton, Washington taught school in Malden and then spent a year at Wayland Seminary in Washington, D.C. His experience here reinforced attitudes which had been inculcated at Hampton. He was somewhat disdainful of the purely academic training offered at Wayland and more firmly convinced of the value of a system which emphasized practical skills, self-help, and the dignity of labor. From Wayland he returned to Hampton for two years as a teacher.

Then in 1881, on the recommendation of General Armstrong, he went to Tuskegee in Macon County, Alabama, to become principal of a new school. The Alabama legislature had authorized the establishment of a normal school to train colored teachers and had appropriated $2,000 for salaries. When Washington arrived, however, there were no buildings, nor even land upon which to build. The school was at first conducted in a shanty loaned by the local Negro church. But, in spite of seemingly insurmountable obstacles, Washington acquired land, built buildings, secured equipment, and recruited teachers and students. The next fifteen years of his life were spent in creating in the Black Belt of Alabama an institution which was in large part a replica of Hampton. There was one significant difference: Hampton had been founded by white persons and the principal and part of the staff were white, while Tuskegee was an all-Negro institution.

The bricks for the buildings at Tuskegee were made by the students, and much of the construction was done by student labor. A large part of the food consumed by the students was grown and prepared by them. In the classrooms academic subjects were infused with materials and examples of a utilitarian nature and related to the actual experience of the students. All boys received "industrial training" in such fields as brickmaking, carpentry, blacksmithing, dairying, and agriculture. Girls studied cooking and sewing. Much emphasis was placed on teaching personal hygiene and manners and on character building. Tuskegee was nondenominational, but all students were required to attend chapel daily and a series of religious services on Sunday. Most impressive were the Sunday evening meetings at which Washington addressed the students.

By 1906 enrollment at Tuskegee had grown to 1,500, and the staff numbered 155. By the time of Washington's death the school had an endowment of about $2 million, property worth more than $1.5 million, and an annual budget of $300,000. In addition to regular classes Tuskegee extended its influence through short courses for farmers, the annual Farmers' Conference, the Rural School Extension Department, and the Tuskegee Negro Conferences. Tuskegee graduates taught in all of the states in the South and in Africa.

Meanwhile, soon after going to Tuskegee, Washington had married his boyhood sweetheart, Fannie N. Smith of Malden. She died two years later, leaving an infant daughter, Portia. In 1885 Washington married Olivia Davidson, who had been assistant principal at Tuskegee and who had contributed almost as much as Washington himself to establishing the school and raising funds during its early years. Two sons, Booker Taliaferro, Jr., and E. Davidson, were born of this marriage. The second Mrs. Washington died in 1889. In 1893 Washington was married a third time—to Margaret Murray, a graduate of Fisk University, who had come to Tuskegee in 1889 as lady principal. She was her husband's enthusiastic supporter in all his endeavors and played an important role at Tuskegee.

From the earliest years at Tuskegee, Washington had gone on northern tours, seeking funds and sometimes making speeches on behalf of his school and explaining his educational doctrines. In 1884 his reputation as a speaker brought him an invitation to address the annual meeting of the National Educational Association at Madison, Wisconsin. But his first important opportunity to speak in the South came when he was designated to give an address on behalf of Negroes at the opening of the Cotton States and International Exposition in Atlanta on September 18, 1895. The speech, given before a racially mixed audience, was directed principally to the white listeners. Although it lasted only about fifteen minutes, it contained the basic ideas on race relations which have ever since been associated with the name of Washington. Both the speech and the speaker were received with tumultuous applause by the audience. White newspapers, North and South, gave the address extended coverage and praised Washington editorially. Almost overnight the principal of Tuskegee found himself a national figure, hailed as spokesman and leader of Negro Americans.

After the address honors came thick and fast. The following year Harvard University conferred an honorary M.A. degree upon Washington, the first such degree it had awarded to a Negro. In 1898 President McKinley visited Tuskegee while on a tour of the South. In 1899 white friends sent Washington on a European tour for a much-needed vacation. Everywhere he went he was lionized. He even had tea with Queen Victoria.

After the Atlanta Address, Washington was in such demand as a public speaker that he spent a substantial part of each year on the lecture circuit. His activities were so fully reported in the press that he became one of the best-known Americans of his day. As his fame increased, there were demands for his autobiography. In 1901 *Up From Slavery* appeared in book form after having first been serialized in *The Outlook*. This account of his trials and successes immediately became a best seller in the United States and was ultimately translated into more than a dozen foreign languages. Emmett Scott, Washington's secretary, later wrote that *Up From Slavery* brought more money to Tuskegee than any other effort of Washington's. It was the reading of this book, more than anything else, which caused Andrew Carnegie and Henry H. Rogers of the Standard Oil Company to become interested in Tuskegee.

In spite of the adulation which was heaped upon him, Washington's position with white southerners was always somewhat precarious. This was vividly demonstrated by the furor which ensued when it became known that President Theodore Roosevelt had entertained the Negro educator at a family dinner at the White House. For weeks —and even months—southern newspapers and southern politicians played up the incident as evidence that Roosevelt and Washington were seeking to break down social barriers between whites and Negroes. But the real significance of the incident was the fact that the President of the United States was consulting with a southern Negro about political matters. Throughout Roosevelt's administration he relied heavily upon Washington's advice in making appointments of whites as well as Negroes in the South and consulted with him on other matters relating to racial policies. Behind the scenes Washington worked for the election of William Howard Taft as Roosevelt's successor in 1908, and he continued to wield important influence during Taft's administration. In spite of his deprecatory attitude toward politics Washington had far greater political power than any other Negro of his time and probably more influence at the White House than any white southerner. But his influence was sharply reduced when Wilson, a Democrat, was elected in 1912.

Washington also showed a remarkable capacity for winning the trust and support of leading industrialists and financiers. Most significant perhaps was his relationship with Andrew Carnegie, who became Tuskegee's most important donor and who bestowed upon Washington a gift of money which guaranteed him and his wife an income for life. Washington was also on friendly terms with William H. Baldwin, Jr., vice-president of the Southern Railway, Henry H. Rogers of Standard Oil, merchants John W. Wanamaker and Robert C. Ogden, Collis P. Huntington, the railroad magnate, and Julius Rosenwald of Sears, Roebuck and Company. Some of these men, although northerners, had interests in the rising industries of the New South, a fact which Washington undoubtedly kept in mind when expressing his views on labor relations and economic policies in general. Washington also successfully cultivated good relations with conservative southern political leaders like Governor Thomas G. Jones of Alabama, whom he persuaded Theodore Roosevelt to appoint to the federal bench. He also knew well such men as Walter Hines Page and Lyman Abbott, who as editors and publishers were influential in molding public opinion. Many of these men served on the board of Tuskegee and gave money to the school. Washington was also instrumental in persuading some of them to endow other agencies for the promotion of Negro education in the South. Among these were the Rockefeller-endowed General Education Board, which was concerned with higher education, and the Rosenwald Fund, the Anna T. Jeanes Fund, and the Phelps-Stokes Fund, all of which were concerned with the education of rural Negroes. It was unlikely that any Negro institution would become a recipient of white philanthropy unless Washington approved.

So great was Washington's influence in the white world that Negroes in politics, education, and other fields were dependent upon his good will for appointments. But at the same time Washington's influence with whites depended in part upon the support which he had from the Negro community. Although always preserving a modest and self-effacing facade, he worked assiduously to maintain his reputation as race leader. He organized the National Negro Business League and served as its president, and for a number of years he dominated the Afro-American Council, an organization dedicated to working against racial discrimination. He used the Negro press and other publications for promoting his ideology and his personal prestige.

But from the time he first won national recognition some Negroes dissented from his doctrines and refused to acknowledge him as the leader of his race. In 1903 the existence of Negro opposition received increasing attention among whites when W. E. B. Du Bois publicly took issue with Washington. Du Bois, who was the first Negro to receive a Ph.D. degree from Harvard, symbolized the Negro intellectuals who were critical of Washington's educational doctrines and his apparent acquiescence in disfranchisement and segregation. Shortly before this, William Monroe Trotter, a Harvard graduate, had begun publication of the Boston *Guardian,* a militant newspaper which has as its *raison d'etre* opposition to Washington and which subjected him to virulent abuse. In 1905 Du Bois, Trotter, and other Negro intellectuals formed the Niagara Movement to fight uncompromisingly for full citizenship for Negroes. More threatening to Washington's position was the founding in 1909 of the National Association for the Advancement of Colored People, a biracial organization in which the white philanthropist Oswald Garrison Villard, who had been a supporter of Tuskegee, played a prominent role. Du Bois became executive secretary of the NAACP and editor of its publication, *The Crisis.*

In the face of rising opposition Washington made strenuous efforts to maintain his position and to discredit his critics. Until his death he continued to enjoy the support of most of the philanthropists and the white press. When he died in 1915, he was eulogized as few Americans have ever been. Nevertheless in his last years, as a result of the rise of the NAACP and the victory of Wilson and the Democrats, the power and prestige which he had wielded diminished somewhat.

His speeches and published writings reveal Washington as a man of a few basic ideas which he constantly reiterated. His fundamental philosophy appears to have crystallized early and to have changed very little. He was a prolific writer, but all his writings say essentially the same thing.

At the outset of his career, Washington later wrote, he recognized that if Tuskegee was to be a success he must win the support of three groups—the "best class" of southern whites, northern whites with a philanthropic interest in the South, and members of his own race. It is evident that in everything he wrote he weighed the effect of his words on these three groups. He was remarkably successful in winning white support, and his success must be attributed in large part to the fact that the views which he expressed on almost all subjects—political, economic, social, as well as racial—were essentially the views of contemporary white Americans. There is little that is original in his thought, and his style is pedestrian and heavy with clichés. At first reading he appears to have been a simple man with simple ideas, but a more careful reading reveals a subtlety not at first apparent. The ambiguity and ambivalence in nearly everything he said or wrote were no doubt the result of the peculiar position he held in relation to whites and Negroes. His writings show little evidence of intellectual or scholarly profundity, but they reveal a man with an understanding of the psychology of the white society in which he lived and with which he had to deal.

He appeared to accept the traditional southern view of the American past, including the Negro past. He once compared the slave system to a prison, but he usually emphasized the benevolent aspects of slavery. He appears to have had no bitter personal memories of his slave origins, and he told many stories of the loyalty of slaves to their masters and the mutual affection between slaves and members of the master's family. He spoke of the "naturally cheerful disposition of the African," and his delineation of "Negro character" corresponded closely with the stereotype accepted by his white contemporaries. Much of his popularity rested on the "darkey" stories with which he delighted white audiences—stories in which the Negro was depicted as a lovable, sometimes shrewd, but essentially childlike figure.

He frequently expressed the opinion, shared by most of his generation, that Reconstruction had been a tragic mistake. In *Up From Slavery* he says that even as a child he felt that Reconstruction policy toward Negroes had rested on a false foundation and was "artificial and forced"—that it was a policy imposed by white northern politicians who "wanted to punish the Southern white men by forcing them [Negroes] into positions over the heads of the Southern whites." It would have been better for the Negro in the long run, he felt, if there had been educational or property requirements for voting. Instead of concentrating on political activity and looking to the federal government for aid and protection, the recently emancipated slaves would have done better to have directed their energies toward securing an education and property.

The core of Washington's philosophy was that the progress of Negroes in all other fields depended upon economic progress. The opportunity to earn a living and acquire property was more important than the right to vote. Throughout his career he tried to impress upon the masses of Negroes that "in agriculture, in industries, in commerce, and in the struggle toward economic success, there were compensations for losses they had suffered in other [i.e. political] directions." Negroes had to learn that "economic efficiency was the foundation for every kind of success." If they made themselves economically indispensable, they would gain political and other rights. "No race that has anything to contribute to the markets of the world is long in any degree ostracized," he said in the Atlanta Address. He frequently asserted that if a Negro held the mortgage on a white man's house it was unlikely that the white man would try to prevent him from voting.

"Cast down your buckets where you are," he advised Negroes in the Atlanta Address, and he continued to the end of his life to insist that Negroes had better economic opportunities in the South and encountered less economic discrimination there than in the North. He also thought that Negroes were better off in the South because there were fewer temptations to immorality and extravagance than in northern cities.

Along with emphasis upon economic progress, he preached the doctrine of thrift and the dignity of labor. He frequently berated Negroes for their tendency to waste their money on "the ornamental gewgaws of life." The opportunity to earn a dollar in a factory was of more importance to the Negro, he said, than the opportunity to spend a dollar in the opera house.

The educational system which he developed at Tuskegee was a natural outgrowth of these views. Slavery had meant work, and in the early years of freedom, said Washington, Negroes had too often looked upon education as means of escaping from work. Tuskegee, like Hampton, stressed the dignity of work and the moral value of working with the hands. Above all, Washington sought to stress the *practical* and to relate the education of the students to the world in which they lived. It was not enough to teach students of the Black Belt out of books. They must also be taught elementary lessons of conduct, including personal cleanliness. Washington laid great stress upon the importance of the toothbrush. "In all my teaching," he said, "I have watched carefully the influence of the toothbrush, and I am convinced that there are few agencies of civilization that are more far-reaching."

Most of the course of study was intended to prepare the students to be successful farmers or artisans or teachers. It was geared to making it possible for them to improve their economic status but not to making them dissatisfied or unable to adjust to the realities of the situation in which southern Negroes lived. "I saw clearly," said Washington, "that an education that filled them with a 'divine discontent,' without ability to change conditions, would leave the students, and the masses they were to guide, worse off than they were in their unawakened state."

Pragmatist (and materialist) that he was, Washington seems to have had little interest in developing the aesthetic interests of his students, and he frequently made disparaging comments about Negroes who studied French grammar or Latin or Greek but who did not have needed vocational skills. These remarks evoked sharp criticism from Negro intellectuals, who insisted that the Tuskegee system was intended to perpetuate a caste system in which Negroes would be nothing more than manual laborers. In reply Washington said that no one system of education was suitable for all Negroes but that industrial training was appropriate for most of them at this particular stage of their development and of the economic development of the South. He admitted that there was a need for Negro colleges to train potential leaders.

On the subject of the political rights of Negroes, as on the subject of education, Washington's statements were somewhat ambiguous and ambivalent. As already noted, he appeared to think that political rights had been too hastily conferred during Reconstruction and that immediate universal suffrage had been unwise. In 1898 he sent an appeal to the Louisiana Constitutional Convention, which was considering disfranchisement. "The Negro agrees with you," he said, "that it is necessary to the salvation of the south that restriction be placed upon the ballot," but he pleaded with the convention to impose the same educational and property requirements on white men as on black men. At the same time he urged the convention to provide greater educational opportunities for Negroes and expressed the hope that "in proportion as the ignorant secure education, property and character, they will be given all the rights of citizenship." In *Up From Slavery* he said it was the duty of the Negro "to deport himself modestly in regard to political claims," and many times thereafter he made disparaging comments about political activity and failed to remonstrate publicly as state after state adopted disfranchisement measures. He sometimes advanced the curious argument that, even though they did not "go through the form of casting the ballot," Negroes who were substantial property owners and respected members of their communities could exert influence on public officials in matters pertaining to race relations almost as effectively as if they had the vote. At the same time he admitted that "in a republican form of government, if any group of people is left permanently without the franchise they are placed at a serious disadvantage."

He seemed honestly to believe that once the Negro had acquired property whites would be willing for him to vote because they would realize that as a property owner and taxpayer he would be a "conservative and safe citizen." He found it gratifying that when Alabama adopted a new constitution disfranchising most Negroes his local registration board sent him a special invitation to register and that the other members of the Tuskegee were permitted to register and vote freely.

Washington was more outspoken on the subject of lynching than on any form of injustice perpetrated on members of his race. In 1904 he made a public appeal through the press for a cessation of this outrageous and brutal disregard for legal processes. And in speech after speech he reiterated the plea. But on the most sensitive issue of all, the social relations between the races, Washington was even more cautious and circumspect than on the question of political rights. "The wisest among my race," he assured his white listeners in the Atlanta Address, "understand that the agitation of questions of social equality is the extremest folly." In his own case, he later remarked, even though he had "opportunities, such as few colored men have had, of getting acquainted with many of the best white people, North and South," this had not caused him to get away from his own people. He was "just as proud of being a Negro as they were of being white people." Elsewhere, in what appeared to be almost an apology for dining at the White House, he said that it was better to "let sleeping dogs lie" and not to disturb existing prejudices. But in an article on "The Negro's Place in American Life," he attempted to show white Americans the lengths to which Negroes were daily compelled to go to avoid crossing the color line and causing friction. At the same time he gently pointed out some of the absurdities which resulted from the drawing of the line.

While acquiescing in separation of the races in all social matters, Washington emphasized that throughout American history the lives of whites and Negroes had been inextricably linked. He told Negroes that their best friends were their white neighbors of the "better class." He constantly tried to persuade southern whites that it was in their own self-interest to help the Negro improve his condition. He stressed the advantages of employing Negroes who were "loyal" and "unresentful." He sometimes spoke disparagingly of labor unions (which did indeed discriminate against Negroes) and of white foreign-born workers. In a speech before a Southern Industrial Convention he reminded his listeners that they were indebted to the black man for labor that was "almost a stranger to strikes, lockouts, and labor wars," and that spoke their language and was never "tempted to follow the red flag of anarchy" but always followed the "safe flag" of the United States and "the spotless banner of the Cross."

But while stressing interdependence and mutuality of interests, Washington also organized the National Negro Business League, which had as its purpose the winning of white respect by developing economic independence from the white community. Through the national organization and local leagues Negroes were encouraged to own and patronize their own businesses.

Washington invariably addressed whites in conciliatory terms. Although all contemporary observers agreed that he possessed great personal dignity and was not servile, some of his language was almost obsequious. He was always quick to praise any evidence, however small, of good will and constructive effort on the part of whites. He did not completely ignore the injustices for which they were responsible but mentioned them so delicately and gently that most of his white audience was probably oblivious of his intent. On the other hand, in speaking to and about members of his own race he was sometimes sharply critical and always laid greater stress on the duties and responsibilities of Negroes than on their rights. White newspapers invariably headlined his rebukes to Negroes. Under the circumstances it is not surprising that both whites and Negroes gained the impression that he thought that the primary responsibility for improving race relations lay with Negroes.

While always preserving an appearance of humility and publicly deprecating the title of "race leader," Washington did indeed see himself in this role. In fact he worked unremittingly to create and preserve the image of himself as leader and spokesman for a Negro community which was virtually unanimous in its support of his policies. While often proclaiming his honesty and frankness in dealing with both whites and Negroes, in reality Washington resorted to devious and clandestine measures to silence or discredit his critics and to maintain his own image of race leader. Especially illuminating were his relations with the Negro press. In discussing his role and his efforts to reach the Negro masses, he wrote that it had been suggested to him that he buy a newspaper or pay papers to promulgate his ideas, but he insisted that he had rejected the suggestion as improper. He flatly denied that he tried to influence the press financially but expressed satisfaction that with a few insignificant exceptions Negro newspapers supported his views. In reality, as recent scholarship has shown, in spite of his protestations to the contrary, Washington was for a number of years part owner of the New York *Age,* the most influential race paper of the period, and subsidized in one way or another a large part of the Negro press. Through these papers he gained not only publicity but favorable editorial comment for himself and unfavorable treatment of his critics.

In his published works he spoke patronizingly of the Negro intellectuals who were critical of him and minimized their attacks. This "small group" opposed him, he contended, because they felt that the southern white man was the natural enemy of the Negro and they regarded his efforts to gain the white man's good will as a "kind of treason to the race." Some of his critics, he suggested, made a business of agitating upon the race question and did not want to see the Negro lose his grievances because they did not want to lose their jobs.[5] Intellectuals, he added, understood theories, read books, and quoted Shakespeare but were unfamiliar with practical matters and understood little about the actual needs of the colored people of the South.

Washington also took issue with his critics because they emphasized the gloomy aspects of the race situation. He himself was invariably optimistic. He dwelt upon the material and educational progress which Negroes had made since emancipation, partly to refute the arguments advanced by some whites that after the removal of the controls and "civilizing" influences of slavery Negroes were retrogressing into barbarism. He lauded any signs of white benevolence and good will. He constantly stressed the blessings of adversity, and after a trip to Europe in 1911 he wrote *The Man Farthest Down* to demonstrate that the conditions and prospects of American Negroes were more favorable than those of the peasants and slum dwellers in Europe.

This persistent optimism stemmed in part from his belief that Negroes would gain more support from white society through a positive, constructive approach to their problems than through emphasizing their grievances. As he told a Negro audience: "No one likes to feel that he is continually following a funeral procession." His cheerful outlook appears also to have been partly the result of his own remarkable personal experience. Whites regarded him as an "exceptional" Negro, and he undoubtedly agreed. Yet he appeared to regard his own success as symbolic of the race. Had not the registrars of Macon County issued him a special invitation to vote? Did he not mingle with the "best" white people in the North? If he could achieve this, could not others?

But the optimism was partly a facade, and in the last years of his life the persistent cheerfulness and the constant eagerness to conciliate whites seemed to diminish somewhat. In some of his last writings he became a little more outspoken on racial injustice. The change in tone may have occurred because he felt sufficiently secure to be more frank, or it may have been that changing times, and especially the rise of the NAACP, caused him to modify his position slightly.

In a new introduction to a reissue of *Up From Slavery* published

---

[5] This was probably a reference to W. E. B. Du Bois, who had recently become the executive secretary of the NAACP.

in 1965, Langston Hughes said that part of the "truth" of Washington's autobiography was its "dissimulation." Rebecca Chalmers Barton observed that Washington wrote "a story of his life which would conform to the white demand for safe and sane Negroes." But Washington's white contemporaries, less analytical than a later generation, failed to recognize the complexity of the man and almost always accepted what he said at face value.

Largely no doubt because he said what they wanted to hear and avoided or minimized the grimmer aspects of the race problem, white Americans generally lauded Washington and endorsed his doctrines. A few leading southern demagogues, notably Ben Tillman and James K. Vardaman, heaped vicious abuse on the Tuskegean for his efforts to educate and uplift Negroes. Some white clergymen and educators argued that Negroes were uneducable and that the only solution to the race problem was deportation. At the time of the White House dinner nearly all of the white newspapers of the South were critical of Washington and some of them vilified him. But on the whole he received extensive and favorable treatment in the white press, North and South, and in the journals of opinion. He was praised because he was a "safe" leader and not an "agitator" and because his approach to the race problem was "constructive." White journals admired him for emphasizing the duties and responsibilities of Negroes more than their "rights." The man himself was frequently characterized as the "Moses of his people" and portrayed as almost saintlike in his humility and charity. At the same time part of his popularity with whites rested on more earthy qualities, especially his humor.

In private correspondence Theodore Roosevelt described Washington as "a genius such as does not arise in a generation," and said that he did not know "a white man of the South who is as good a man as Booker Washington today." [6] Andrew Carnegie thought he was "certainly one of the most wonderful men living or who has ever lived." Walter Hines Page had worried long over the evil results of slavery and the inability of statesmen to find an answer to the race problem. But after a visit to Tuskegee he realized that the "way out of a century of blunders" had been found by Washington, "who had shown the way." William Dean Howells was only slightly

[3] Roosevelt to Owen Wister, April 26, 1906, Elting E. Morison, ed., *The Letters of Theodore Roosevelt*, 8 vols. (Cambridge, Mass., 1951–54), V, 227; Roosevelt to Julius Rosenwald, December 15, 1915, *ibid.*, VIII, 997.

less eulogistic. He thought the Tuskegeean inferior intellectually to Frederick Douglass but described him as an "exemplary citizen," whose "adroit . . . subtle statesmanship" was the only realistic method of dealing with the race situation in his own time.

One of the few contemporary writers who attempted to probe behind Washington's inscrutably optimistic facade was H. G. Wells, who traveled in the United States in 1905 and wrote an article entitled "The Tragedy of Color" as part of a series on conditions in America. What struck Wells most forcibly about Washington was the way in which "the sense of the overpowering forces of race prejudice" weighed upon him. He made one feel, said Wells, "with an exaggerated intensity" the "monstrous injustice" of prejudice even though he refused to discuss it openly. Because race prejudice was the central fact of Washington's life, he "dreamed of a colored race of decent and inaggressive men silently giving the lie to all the legend of their degradation" by winning success as doctors, lawyers, and businessmen. But, asked Wells, would uneducated whites endure "even so submissive vindication" as the one which Washington envisioned? Would they not resent prosperous, self-respecting Negroes?

Another white writer less sympathetic to the plight of the Negro than Wells asked the same question. He was Thomas Dixon, a Baptist minister turned novelist, who propagated racism through such books as *The Clansman*. In an article published in 1905 Dixon professed to have the warmest admiration for Washington but denied emphatically that his program would solve the Negro problem. On the contrary, education would drive the races further apart. "If there is one thing a Southern white man cannot endure," said Dixon, "it is an educated negro." The Tuskegeean's efforts to make the Negro into a potential competitor with the white man would have disastrous results. Moreover, said Dixon, Washington was in reality silently preparing the way for the assimilation and amalgamation of the races; either this or something equally dangerous—a separate Negro nation within a nation. For his consummate skill in evading the issue of his real aims Dixon dubbed Washington "the greatest diplomat his race has ever produced."

Inevitably many writers compared Washington and Du Bois as symbols of two types of Negro leaders. Even those who admired Du Bois' intellectual and literary abilities usually endorsed Washington's "constructive" approach with its emphasis upon gradualism and duties and responsibilities and deplored Du Bois' bitterness and militancy. A correspondent of the Chicago *Tribune,* writing in 1906, deplored the increasing influence of Du Bois among Negroes.

> Most white people, of course, believe that Booker T. Washington has taken hold of the problem at the right end . . . If the colored people gave Booker Washington anything like the support the white people do there would probably be no race problem in this country. The blacks would settle down to do the things they are fitted to do at the present time and they would gradually raise themselves in the social and political scale as they acquired education, general intelligence and consequent self-reliance.[7]

It is difficult to determine what Washington's Negro contemporaries really thought of him. The great mass of Negroes living in the rural South were largely inarticulate. However, it seems reasonable to assume that many of them admired him if only because he was a southern Negro who had gained fame as well as because he preached doctrines and a program which they could understand. But the sincerity of comment on Washington in much of the Negro press and by Negro politicians and other leaders is always somewhat suspect because of his efforts to subsidize and influence the press and his control over political appointments and donations to educational institutions. Undoubtedly some praised him publicly while secretly disagreeing with him, while others remained silent instead of criticizing him openly. But he was never able to control completely the editorial comment even of the publications which he subsidized. And it seems probable that many of the men who endorsed his views would have done so even if he had not sought their support.

For many years one of Washington's closest confidants and most loyal supporters was T. Thomas Fortune, editor of the New York *Age,* who was regarded as the most able Negro journalist of the period. Fortune was always much the more militant of the two, but he praised Washington as the strongest and safest of race leaders and emphasized that an important source of his strength was that he enjoyed the confidence of whites in the North and South.

Some Negroes, however, assailed Washington *because* of his white support. Most extreme among his critics was William Monroe Trotter of the Boston *Guardian,* who declared that if Washington was the

---

[7] *Chicago Daily Tribune,* October 27, 1906.

"leader" of colored Americans it was because he was "chosen for that position by the white American race" and that Washington had "always gone out of his way to say things that would suit prejudiced or race-proud white people." He had "ridiculed the right and privilege of suffrage," said Trotter, "had found . . . much to praise in debasing human slavery," and had "aided and abetted the closing of the door of hope and of high opportunity to the Negro race South."

Another bitter critic of Washington was Ida Wells Barnett, wife of the Chicago attorney, Ferdinand Barnett, and one of the founders of the NAACP. As a young woman, she had been forced to leave Memphis because of her outspoken condemnation of lynching. Like many other Negro intellectuals she resented the jokes which Washington told and his gibes at college-educated Negroes. She accused him of reinforcing the unspoken belief of most whites that Negroes were innately inferior and hence not fitted for higher education. As a result of his influence, white philanthropists gave their money to Tuskegee and refused to give money to institutions which stressed academic education.

A more moderate position was taken by the novelist Charles W. Chesnutt. Chesnutt paid tribute to Washington's "eminent services in the cause of education" although he was mildly critical and satirical concerning his overemphasis on industrial training. But as an uncompromising champion of political rights for Negroes, the novelist spoke more sharply about some of Washington's remarks on suffrage. "To try to read anything good into these fraudulent Southern constitutions" which disfranchised Negroes, he said, was "to condone a crime against one's race." But Chesnutt approved of Washington's efforts to win the support of the white South for the Negro's aspirations. Unlike Trotter, Mrs. Barnett, and other militant intellectuals, he maintained friendly personal relations with the Tuskegeean.

W. E. B. Du Bois was Washington's most able and effective critic. After trying to cooperate for a number of years, or at least to avoid an open rupture, in 1903 Du Bois, then at Atlanta University, published an essay, "Of Mr. Booker T. Washington and Others." In it he paid tribute to Washington's "singleness of vision and thorough oneness with his age" and his remarkable success in presenting a program which won the support of the white North and the white South and which "silenced if it did not convert the Negroes themselves." But, he said, in spite of Washington's prestige, educated Negroes were apprehensive of the ascendancy he had gained and the time had come for "honest and earnest criticism." The Tuskegeean's program, he said, "practically accepts the alleged inferiority of the Negro races." Instead of resisting increasing prejudice and oppression, Washington preached submission to loss of political and civil rights and denial of opportunities for higher education. "In the history of nearly all other races and peoples," said Du Bois, "the doctrine preached at such crises [of intensified oppression] has been that manly self-respect is worth more than lands and houses, and that a people who voluntarily surrender such respect, or cease striving for it, are not worth civilizing." The fallacy of Washington's emphasis on economic progress as the key to all progress by Negroes was that under modern competitive conditions it was impossible for Negro workers and property owners to defend their economic rights without the right of suffrage. Black men, said Du Bois, had "a duty stern and delicate" to oppose Washington when he apologized for injustice, when he did not "rightly value the privilege and duty of voting," and when he opposed "the higher training and ambition of our brighter minds."

In a later autobiographical account of his relations with Washington, Du Bois emphasized another reason for opposition to his leadership—the influence of what he called the Tuskegee Machine. By this he meant the power which Washington and his associates exercised over appointments and white philanthropy and over the Negro press.

In the more than half a century which has elapsed since his death a number of writers—usually historians or sociologists—have attempted to evaluate Washington's place in history. The question of whether he was a genuine race leader or merely a mouthpiece for white America has been debated, and inevitably writers have continued to make comparisons between the ideology and leadership of Washington and Du Bois.

In 1916 there appeared *Booker T. Washington, Builder of a Civilization*. The authors were Emmett J. Scott, Washington's longtime secretary, and Lyman Beecher Stowe, who had been commissioned to write the book before Washington's death. Needless to say it was highly laudatory of the man and his doctrines. A few years later in *The Negro in Our History*, Carter G. Woodson, a Negro intellectual and virtually the founder of the study of Negro history, praised Washington's achievements as an educator and said that his silence on the rights of Negroes "did not necessarily mean that he was in favor of the oppression of the race." But he admitted that many Negroes regarded Washington's policy as one of "surrender" to "oppressors who desired to reduce the whole race to menial service."

Writing just ten years after his death, Horace M. Bond, another Negro historian, asserted that during his lifetime Washington had been a real leader of southern Negroes, reaching the masses as Du Bois and his circle were unable to do. But by 1925, although Negro newspapers continued to revere the name of Washington, they no longer espoused his views but preached the more militant doctrines of Du Bois, whose influence was in the ascendancy in all fields of Negro thought. The Washington movement and ideology, said Bond, were "practically sterile." He attributed the rapid decline of the Tuskegeean's influence to two factors. In the first place Washington had left no successor comparable to himself in personality and ability. Secondly, with the mass migration of Negroes from the South to northern cities which began during the First World War, the conditions prevailing during Washington's lifetime had altered drastically. Negroes were ignoring his advice to stay in the South, and in the North they were beginning to be politically active as never before.

Writing in the 1930's Merle Curti, one of the pioneers in studies of American intellectual history, emphasized, as did later writers, that Washington's doctrines and values were those of contemporary America. His "social philosophy was, in fine, more typical of middle-class white Americans, whom he wanted his people to be like, than it was of the Negro as such."

The Great Depression of the 1930's, which hit Negroes more severely than any other sector of the population, caused some scholars to re-examine Washington's doctrines, especially his emphasis on economic factors. Guy B. Johnson, a leading sociologist, said that Washington was the "only Negro leader, who has ever had anything like a race-wide following," while at the same time admitting that he was "in some respects a greater leader of white opinion than he was of Negro opinion." By the 1930's, Johnson said, although it was evident that the NAACP had won some important legal battles, it was doubtful whether the condition of southern Negroes had really improved. The depression made Negroes more acutely aware than ever before of their economic insecurity. He predicted that in the future two types of Negro movements would develop. One would be a "neo-Washington" approach; the other would be communism.

On the other hand, W. Edward Farrison said that the record showed the inadequacy of Washington's program. In spite of the great industrial and material progress of the South since Washington's death, Negroes still lived in poverty and ignorance. The inherent weakness of Washington's approach, he said, was the failure to recognize that without political power the Negro lacked the means to improve his economic status. "Because of a lack of influence and power in the body politic, he can work only at such jobs as are *given* to him."

One of the most perceptive efforts at analyzing and evaluating Washington's role was made by the Swedish economist-sociologist Gunnar Myrdal in *An American Dilemma,* his monumental study of American Negroes published in 1944. Myrdal characterized Washington as a "supreme diplomat" and probably the greatest Negro *politician* in the history of the United States. He was entirely realistic in his approach, especially in his efforts to win the good will of the white South since "it is a political axiom that Negroes can never, in any period, hope to attain more in the *short-term power bargain* than the most benevolent white groups are prepared to give them." But Myrdal questioned Washington's long-range statesmanship, since his virtual monopoly of leadership restricted agitation by Negroes of the Du Bois school who were interested in emphasizing long-range objectives of complete equality.

A different conclusion was reached by Basil Mathews, who attempted to write the first scholarly biography of Washington. In a book published in 1948, which was as eulogistic as any of the accounts written during Washington's lifetime, he asserted that history had vindicated Washington's statesmanship and strategy. But in *The Origins of the New South, 1877–1913,* one of the most significant books on the period ever published, Vann Woodward made an evaluation of the role of Washington and the effects of the Atlanta Compromise which more nearly coincided with Myrdal's views. Woodward asserted that the Tuskegeean's great reputation was not due so much to "the genius and personal influence of Booker Washington as to the remarkable congeniality between his doctrines and the dominant forces of his age and society, forces that found an eloquent voice in the brown orator, but that would have made themselves felt in any case." The Washington program and educational system were inadequate because they looked to the past rather than to the needs of the twentieth century.

Chronology of the Life of Booker T. Washington

1856	(April 5) Born in Franklin County, Virginia, son of a slave Jane and unknown white father.
1865	End of Civil War. Adoption of Thirteenth Amendment abolishing slavery.
1865	Moves with mother and stepfather to Malden, West Virginia.
1865–71	Works in salt mines and coal mines in Malden.
1871–72	Works as houseboy in home of Mrs. Lewis Ruffner.
1872–75	Attends Hampton Normal and Agricultural Institute, graduating with honors in 1875.
1875–78	Teaches school in Malden, West Virginia.
1877	End of Reconstruction Era in South.
1878–79	Attends Wayland Seminary, Washington, D.C.
1879–81	Teaches at Hampton Institute.
1881	Founds and becomes first principal of Tuskegee Institute, Tuskegee, Alabama.
1882	Marries Fannie N. Smith of Malden, West Virginia (d. 1884).
1883	Supreme Court decision in Civil Rights Cases.
1884	Delivers address, "The Educational Outlook in the South," before the National Educational Association at Madison, Wisconsin.
1885	Marries Olivia A. Davidson of Ohio (d. 1889).
1892	First Annual Tuskegee Negro Conference.
1893	Marries Margaret James Murray of Mississippi.
1895	(September 18) Delivers address as Negro representative at opening of Cotton States and International Exposition at Atlanta, Georgia.
1896	Supreme Court decision in *Plessy v. Ferguson* upholds state segregation law.
1896	Speaks at Harvard University Commencement and receives honorary M.A. degree from Harvard.
1898	(February) Appeals to Louisiana Constitutional Convention on subject of Negro disfranchisement.
1898	(December) President William McKinley visits Tuskegee.
1899	Visits Europe.

1900	Organizes National Negro Business League.
1901	Publishes *Up From Slavery*.
1901	Receives honorary Doctor's degree from Dartmouth College.
1901	(October) White House Dinner. President Theodore Roosevelt consults with Washington about political appointments in the South.
1902	William Monroe Trotter begins publication of Boston *Guardian*, attacking Washington as race leader.
1903	W. E. B. Du Bois publishes "Of Mr. Booker T. Washington and Others," in *Souls of Black Folk*, publicly criticizing Washington.
1905	Founding of Niagara Movement.
1909	Founding of the National Association for the Advancement of Colored People.
1911	Publishes *My Larger Education*.
1911	Travels in Europe.
1912	Publishes *The Man Farthest Down*.
1915	(November 14) Dies at Tuskegee, Alabama.

PART ONE

BOOKER T. WASHINGTON LOOKS AT THE WORLD

During the period of Washington's pre-eminence, from the Atlanta Address in 1895 until his death in 1915, a steady stream of books and articles issued from Tuskegee, and he delivered countless speeches.[1] But much of his writing and oratory was repetitive. In certain respects a slight change in emphasis was apparent in his later years, but, on the whole, his ideology and program of racial adjustment remained essentially the same throughout his career.

The editor has attempted to make selections which illustrate his philosophy, his proposals for solving race problems, and his views on his role as race leader. Included are parts of his two principal autobiographical works, Up From Slavery *and* "Chapters from My Experience," [2] *and excerpts from his other books and articles and his speeches.*

1

The Negro Past

In the passages below Washington expressed views on the Negro past similar to those of the white historians and other white writers of his era. While denying that he was an apologist for slavery, he stressed the civilizing and benevolent aspects of the institution. Many of the policies of Reconstruction were, he felt, a mistake. It would have been wiser to put less emphasis upon political activity and to have imposed educational or property tests for voting.

[1] See Bibliographical Note for the assistance which Washington received from "ghost writers" and others in the preparation of his publications.

[2] "Chapters from My Experience" was published in book form as *My Larger Experience* (New York, 1911).

THE SCHOOL OF SLAVERY [3]

I pity from the bottom of my heart any nation or body of people that is so unfortunate as to get entangled in the net of slavery. I have long since ceased to cherish any spirit of bitterness against the Southern white people on account of the enslavement of my race. No one section of our country was wholly responsible for its introduction and, besides, it was recognized and protected for years by the General Government. Having once got its tentacles fastened on to the economic and social life of the Republic, it was no easy matter for the country to relieve itself of the institution. Then, when we rid ourselves of prejudice, or racial feeling, and look facts in the face, we must acknowledge that, notwithstanding the cruelty and moral wrong of slavery, the ten million Negroes inhabiting this country, who themselves or whose ancestors went through the school of American slavery, are in a stronger and more hopeful condition, materially, intellectually, morally, and religiously, than is true of an equal number of black people in any other portion of the globe. This is so to such an extent that Negroes in this country, who themselves or whose forefathers went through the school of slavery, are constantly returning to Africa as missionaries to enlighten those who remained in the fatherland. This I say, not to justify slavery—on the other hand, I condemn it as institution, as we all know that in America it was established for selfish and financial reasons, and not from a missionary motive—but to call attention to a fact, and to show how Providence so often uses men and institutions to accomplish a purpose. . . .

Ever since I have been old enough to think for myself, I have entertained the idea that, notwithstanding the cruel wrongs inflicted upon us, the black man got nearly as much out of slavery as the white man did. The hurtful influences of the institution were not by any means confined to the Negro. This was fully illustrated by the life upon our own plantation. The whole machinery of slavery was so constructed as to cause labour, as a rule, to be looked upon as a badge of degradation, of inferiority. Hence labour was something that both races on the slave plantation sought to escape. The slave system on our place, in a large measure, took the spirit of self-reliance and self-help out of the white people.

[3] *Up From Slavery: An Autobiography* (New York, 1901), pp. 16–17.

NEGRO'S LIFE IN SLAVERY [4]

The Negro in exile from his native land neither pined away nor grew bitter. On the contrary, as soon as he was able to adjust himself to the conditions of his new life, his naturally cheerful and affectionate disposition began to assert itself. Gradually the natural human sympathies of the African began to take root in the soil of the New World, and then, growing up spontaneously, to twine about the life of the white man, by whose side the black man now found himself. The slave soon learned to love the children of his master, and they loved him in return. The quaint humor of the Negro slave helped him to turn many a hard corner. It helped to excuse his mistakes, and, by turning a reproof into a jest, to soften the resentment of his master for his faults. . . .

I have frequently met and talked with old men of my race who have grown up in slavery. . . .

One old farmer who owns a thousand acres of land not far from Tuskegee said: "We's jes' so ign't out heah, we don' see no diff'rence 'twe'n freedom an' slav'ry, 'cept den we's workin' fer some one else, and now we's workin' fer oursel's."

Some time ago an old colored man who has lived for a number of years near the Tuskegee Institute, in talking about his experience since freedom, remarked that the greatest difference he had found between slavery and freedom was that in the days of slavery his master had to think for him, but since he had been free he had to think and plan for himself. . . .

There was much in slavery besides its hardships and its cruelties; much that was tender, human, and beautiful. The heroic efforts that many of the slaves made to buy their own and their children's freedom deserve to be honored equally with the devotion that they frequently showed in the service of their masters. And, after all, considering the qualities which the Negro slave developed under trying conditions, it does not seem to me that there is any real reason why any one who wishes him well should despair of the future of the Negro either in this country or elsewhere.

[4] "The Negro's Life in Slavery," *The Outlook*, XCIII (September 11, 1909), 74–78. This article was later incorporated into *The Story of the Negro*, 2 vols. (New York, 1909).

SOUTHERN WHITES AND SLAVERY [5]

One of the first results of the presence of the Negro in America, for example, was the building up in a free country of a system of slavery; and one of the first effects of slavery was to emphasize and bring to the surface in the life of the stronger race two qualities or sets of qualities, one good and the other bad, one of which tended to degrade the Negro and the other to lift him up and civilize him. These two sets of qualities eventually became embodied in two types or classes of individuals.

One of these was known as the "poor whites"; the other was the Southern aristocracy. It was from the ranks of the "poor whites" that the majority of the overseers, the men who performed all the brutal and degrading work connected with slavery, were drawn. It was this class that was most injured by the effects of slavery; and it was but natural, perhaps, that the men of this class should have come to have the most bitter hatred of the black man. . . .

On the other hand, members of the old Southern families were brought in the daily lives of their homes into intimate human relationship with the black people about them, and, as a consequence, grew to feel a deep sympathy with and responsibility for the slaves under their care. Many of these people deplored the system in which they found themselves fatally entangled. Many of them freed their slaves, and many more would gladly have done so if they had felt that freedom would have solved the problem which the system of slavery had created. I have always felt that the best and truest friend of the Negro in freedom has been that Southern white man who, in slavery days, gained an intimate and personal acquaintance with the Negro in the way that I have described.

In saying this I do not intend to make any apology for the system of slavery, nor do I pretend that I have always shared the views in regard to the Negro that are usually held by the former slaveholders.

THE RECONSTRUCTION PERIOD [6]

During the whole of the Reconstruction period our people throughout the South looked to the Federal Government for every-

[5] "Chapters from My Experience," *World's Work*, XXI (January, 1911), 13848.
[6] *Up From Slavery*, pp. 83–85.

thing, very much as a child looks to its mother. This was not un-
natural. The central government gave them freedom, and the whole
Nation had been enriched for more than two centuries by the labour
of the Negro. Even as a youth, and later in manhood, I had the
feeling that it was cruelly wrong in the central government, at the
beginning of our freedom, to fail to make some provision for the
general education of our people in addition to what the states might
do, so that the people would be the better prepared for the duties
of citizenship.

It is easy to find fault, to remark what might have been done, and
perhaps, after all, and under all the circumstances, those in charge
of the conduct of affairs did the only thing that could be done at the
time. Still, as I look back now over the entire period of our freedom,
I cannot help feeling that it would have been wiser if some plan
could have been put in operation which would have made the possession of a certain amount of education or property, or both, a test
for the exercise of the franchise, and a way provided by which this
test should be made to apply honestly and squarely to both the white
and black races.

Though I was but little more than a youth during the period of
Reconstruction, I had the feeling that mistakes were being made, and
that things could not remain in the condition that they were in then
very long. I felt that the Reconstruction policy, so far as it related
to my race, was in a large measure on a false foundation, was artificial
and forced. In many cases it seemed to me that the ignorance of
my race was being used as a tool with which to help white men into
office, and that there was an element in the North which wanted to
punish the Southern white men by forcing the Negro into positions
over the heads of the Southern whites. I felt that the Negro would
be the one to suffer for this in the end. Besides, the general political
agitation drew the attention of our people away from the more
fundamental matters of perfecting themselves in the industries at their
doors and in securing property.

2

The Atlanta Address[1]

In this speech, which made him a national figure, Washington expressed the essentials of his economic philosophy and his views on the relations between the races. The most famous part is the passage in which he asserted that, although the economic interests of whites and Negroes are interdependent, in social relations the two races can be separate as the fingers on the hand.

Mr. President, Gentlemen of the Board of Directors, and Citizens:

One-third of the population of the South is of Negro race. No enterprise seeking the material, civil, or moral welfare of this section can disregard this element of our population and reach the highest success. I but convey to you, Mr. President and Directors, the sentiment of the masses of my race, when I say that in no way have the value and manhood of the American Negro been more fittingly and generously recognized, than by the managers of this magnificent Exposition at every stage of its progress. It is a recognition which will do more to cement the friendship of the two races than any occurrence since the dawn of our freedom.

Not only this, but the opportunity here afforded will awaken among us a new era of industrial progress. Ignorant and inexperienced, it is not strange that in the first years of our new life we began at the top instead of the bottom; that a seat in Congress or the State Legislature was more sought than real estate or industrial skill; that the political convention or stump speaking had more attractions than starting a dairy farm or truck garden.

A ship lost at sea for many days suddenly sighted a friendly vessel. From the mast of the unfortunate vessel was seen the signal: "Water,

---

[1] *The Negro and the Atlanta Exposition* (Baltimore: Trustees of the John F. Slater Fund, *Occasional Papers*, No. 7, 1896), pp. 12–15.

water, we die of thirst." The answer from the friendly vessel at once came back, "Cast down your bucket where you are." A second time the signal, "Water, water, send us water," ran up from the distressed vessel and was answered, "Cast down your bucket where you are," and a third and fourth signal for water was answered, "Cast down your bucket where you are." The captain of the distressed vessel, at last heeding the injunction, cast down his bucket and it came up full of fresh, sparkling water from the mouth of the Amazon River. To those of my race who depend on bettering their condition in a foreign land, or who underestimate the importance of cultivating friendly relations with the Southern white man who is their next door neighbor, I would say cast down your bucket where you are, cast it down in making friends, in every manly way, of the people of all races by whom we are surrounded. Cast it down in agriculture, in mechanics, in commerce, in domestic service, and in the professions. And in this connection it is well to bear in mind that, whatever other sins the South may be called upon to bear, when it comes to business pure and simple it is in the South that the negro is given a man's chance in the commercial world; and in nothing is this Exposition more eloquent than in emphasising this chance. Our greatest danger is that, in the great gap from slavery to freedom, we may overlook the fact that the masses of us are to live by the productions of our hands, and fail to keep in mind that we shall prosper in proportion as we learn to dignify and glorify common labor and put brains and skill into the common occupations of life; shall prosper in proportion as we learn to draw the line between the superficial and the substantial, the ornamental gewgaws of life and the useful. No race can prosper till it learns that there is as much dignity in tilling a field as in writing a poem. It is at the bottom of life we must begin and not the top. Nor should we permit our grievances to overshadow our opportunities.

To those of the white race who look to the incoming of those of foreign birth and strange tongue and habits for the prosperity of the South, were I permitted, I would repeat what I say to my own race, "Cast down your bucket where you are." Cast it down among the 8,000,000 negroes whose habits you know, whose loyalty and love you have tested in days when to have proved treacherous meant the ruin of your firesides. Cast it down among these people who have, without strikes and labor wars, tilled your fields, cleared your forests, builded your railroads and cities, and brought forth treasures from the bowels of the earth and helped make possible this magnificent representation of the progress of the South. Casting down your bucket among my people, helping and encouraging them as you are doing on these grounds, and to education of head, hand, and heart, you will find that they will buy your surplus land, make blossom the waste places in your fields, and run your factories. While doing this you can be sure in the future, as you have been in the past, that you and your families will be surrounded by the most patient, faithful, law-abiding, and unresentful people that the world has seen. As we have proved our loyalty to you in the past, in nursing your children, watching by the sick beds of your mothers and fathers, and often following them with tear-dimmed eyes to their graves, so in the future, in our humble way, we shall stand by you with a devotion that no foreigner can approach, ready to lay down our lives, if need be, in defense of yours; interlacing our industrial, commercial, civil, and religious life with yours in a way that shall make the interests of both races one. In all things that are purely social we can be as separate as the fingers, yet one as the hand in all things essential to mutual progress.

There is no defense or security for any of us except in the highest intelligence and development of all. If anywhere there are efforts tending to curtail the fullest growth of the negro, let these efforts be turned into stimulating, encouraging, and making him the most useful and intelligent citizen. . . .

Nearly sixteen millions of hands will aid you pulling the load upwards, or they will pull against you the load downwards. We shall constitute one-third and much more of the ignorance and crime of the South, or one-third its intelligence and progress; we shall contribute one-third to the business and industrial prosperity of the South, or we shall prove a veritable body of death, stagnating, depressing, retarding every effort to advance the body politic.

Gentlemen of the Exposition: As we present to you our humble effort at an exhibition of our progress, you must not expect over much; starting thirty years ago with ownership here and there in a few quilts and pumpkins and chickens, (gathered from miscellaneous sources) remember, the path that has led us from these to the invention and production of agricultural implements, buggies, steam engines, newspapers, books, statuary, carvings, paintings, the management of drug stores and banks, has not been trodden without contact with thorns and thistles. While we take pride in what we exhibit as a result of our independent efforts, we do not for a moment forget that our part in this exhibit would fall far short of your expectations but for the constant help that has come to our educational life, not only from the Southern States, but especially from Northern philanthropists who have made their gifts a constant stream of blessing and encouragement.

The wisest among my race understand that the agitation of questions of social equality is the extremest folly, and that progress in the enjoyment of all the privileges that will come to us must be the result of severe and constant struggle, rather than of artificial forcing. No race that has anything to contribute to the markets of the world is long in any degree ostracized. It is important and right that all privileges of the law be ours, but it is vastly more important that we be prepared for the exercise of these privileges. The opportunity to earn a dollar in a factory just now is worth infinitely more than the opportunity to spend a dollar in an opera house.

In conclusion, may I repeat, that nothing in thirty years has given us more hope and encouragement and drawn us so near to you of the white race as the opportunity offered by this Exposition; and here bending, as it were, over the altar that represents the results of the struggles of your race and mine, both starting practically empty-handed three decades ago, I pledge that, in your effort to work out the great and intricate problem which God has laid at the doors of the South, you shall have at all times the patient, sympathetic help of my race. Only let this be constantly in mind, that while, from representations in these buildings of the products of field, of forest, of mine, of factory, letters and art much good will come,—yet, far above and beyond material benefit, will be that higher good, that let us pray God will come, in a blotting out of sectional differences and racial animosities and suspicions, and in a determination, even in the remotest corner, to administer absolute justice; in a willing obedience among all classes to the mandates of law, and a spirit that will tolerate nothing but the highest equity in the enforcement of law. This, this, coupled with material prosperity, will bring into our beloved South a new heaven and a new earth.

3
Educational Philosophy

Washington's educational philosophy was above all pragmatic, stressing the importance of relating education to life. The Tuskegee system of "industrial" or vocational training was designed to fit Negroes to live in the South and improve their economic condition but not to make them discontented with conditions which they could not change. It included such basic matters as training in personal cleanliness and correct behavior. In defending industrial education Washington frequently made disparaging comments about academic training and higher education for Negroes, as illustrated in the selection "Academic Frills." In answer to criticism from Negro intellectuals he replied, in the final selection, that industrial education was not the only system for Negroes and admitted that there was increasing need for institutions of higher learning to train leaders and professional persons.

MORAL VALUES OF HAND WORK [1]

Soon after I was made free by the proclamation of Abraham Lincoln, there came the new opportunity to attend a public school at my home town in West Virginia. When the teacher said that the chief purpose of education was to enable one to speak and write the English language correctly, the statement found lodgment in my mind and stayed there. While at the time I could not put my thoughts into words clearly enough to express instinctive disagreement with my teacher, this definition did not seem adequate, it grated harshly upon my young ears, and I had reasons for feeling that education ought to do more for a person than merely teach him to read and write. While this scheme of education was being held up before me, my mother was living in abject poverty, lacking the commonest necessities of life, and

[1] *Working with the Hands: Being a Sequel to Up From Slavery* (New York, 1904), pp. 3–5.

working day and night to give me a chance to go to school for two or three months of the year. And my foremost aim in going to school was to learn ways and means by which I might make life more endurable, and if possible even attractive, for my mother.

There were several boys of our neighborhood who had superior school advantages, and who, in more than one instance, had reached the point where they were called "educated," which meant they could write and talk correctly. But their parents were not far removed from the conditions in which my mother was living, and I could not help wondering whether this kind of education alone was fitted to help me in the immediate needs of relieving the hard times at home. This idea, however, ran counter to the current widespread opinion among my people. Young as I was, I had come to have the feeling that to be a free boy meant to a considerable extent, freedom from work with the hands, and that this new status applied especially to the educated boy.

Just after the Civil War the Negro lad was strongly influenced by two beliefs: one, that freedom from slavery brought with it freedom from hard work, the other that education of the head would bring even more sweeping emancipation from work with the hands.

EDUCATION MUST HAVE PRACTICAL VALUE [2]

In our industrial teaching we keep three things in mind: first, that the student shall be so educated that he shall be enabled to meet conditions as they exist *now*, in the part of the South where he lives— in a word, to be able to do the thing which the world wants done; second, that every student who graduates from the school shall have enough skill, coupled with intelligence and moral character, to enable him to make a living for himself and others; third, to send every graduate out feeling and knowing that labour is dignified and beautiful—to make each one love labour instead of trying to escape it.

The idea uppermost in my mind, when I began the work of establishing the school at Tuskegee, was to do something that would reach and improve the condition of the masses of the Negro people in the South. Up to that time—and even to-day to a large extent—education had not touched, in any real and tangible way, the great majority

[2] *Up From Slavery: An Autobiography* (New York, 1901), p. 312; "Tuskegee: A Retrospect and Prospect," *North American Review*, CLXXXII (April, 1906), 514–15, 519.

cf the people in what is known as "The Black Belt." I had not been many days in Alabama before I realized this fact. As my knowledge of conditions grew, I became increasingly convinced that any institution which was to be of real service to the millions of the lower South must not confine itself to methods that were suited to some distant community where conditions of life were vastly different. . . .

From the very outset of my work, it has been my steadfast purpose to establish an institution that would provide instruction, not for the select few, but for the masses, giving them standards and ideals, and inspiring in them hope and courage to go patiently forward. I wanted to give Negro young men and women an education that would fit them to take up and carry to greater perfection the work that their fathers and mothers had been doing. I saw clearly that an education that filled them with a "divine discontent," without ability to change conditions, would leave the students, and the masses they were to guide, worse off than they were in their unawakened state. It was my aim to teach the students who came to Tuskegee to live a life and to make a living, to the end that they might return to their homes after graduation, and find profit and satisfaction in building up the communities from which they had come, and in developing the latent possibilities of the soil and the people. . . .

I do not care to venture here an opinion about the nature of knowledge in general; but it will be pretty clear to any one who reflects upon the matter that the only kind of knowledge that has any sort of value for a race that is trying to get on its feet is knowledge that has some definite relation to the daily lives of the men and women who are seeking it.

GOSPEL OF THE TOOTHBRUSH [3]

One thing that I have always insisted upon at Tuskegee is that everywhere there should be absolute cleanliness. Over and over again the students were reminded in those first years—and are reminded now—that people would excuse us for our poverty, for our lack of comforts and conveniences, but that they would not excuse us for dirt.

Another thing that has been insisted upon at the school is the use of the tooth-brush. "The gospel of the tooth-brush," as General Arm-

---

[3] *Up From Slavery*, pp. 174–75. The story about the toothbrush, which Washington frequently told to white audiences, was especially offensive to Negro intellectuals.

strong used to call it, is a part of our creed at Tuskegee. No student is permitted to remain who does not keep and use a tooth-brush. Several times, in recent years, students have come to us who brought with them almost no other article except a tooth-brush. They had heard from the lips of older students about our insisting upon the use of this, and so, to make a good impression, they brought at least a tooth-brush with them. I remember that one morning, not long ago, I went with the lady principal on her usual morning tour of inspection of the girls' rooms. We found one room that contained three girls who had recently arrived at the school. When I asked them if they had tooth-brushes, one of the girls replied, pointing to a brush: "Yes, sir. That is our brush. We bought it together, yesterday." It did not take them long to learn a different lesson.

It has been interesting to note the effect that the use of the tooth-brush has had in bringing about a higher degree of civilization among the students. With few exceptions, I have noticed that, if we can get a student to the point where when the first or second tooth-brush disappears, he of his own motion buys another, I have not been disappointed in the future of that individual.

ACADEMIC FRILLS [4]

When a mere boy, I saw a young colored man, who had spent several years in school, sitting in a common cabin in the South, studying a French grammar. I noted the poverty, the untidiness, the want of system and thrift, that existed about the cabin, notwithstanding his knowledge of French and other academic subjects. Another time, when riding on the outer edges of a town in the South, I heard the sound of a piano coming from a cabin of the same kind. Contriving some excuse, I entered, and began a conversation with the young colored woman who was playing, and who had recently returned from a boarding-school, where she had been studying instrumental music among other things. Despite the fact that her parents were living in a rented cabin, eating poorly cooked food, surrounded with poverty, and having almost none of the conveniences of life, she had persuaded them to rent a piano for four or five dollars per month. Many such instances as these, in connection with my own struggles, impressed upon me the

[4] "The Awakening of the Negro," *The Atlantic Monthly,* LXXVIII (September, 1896), 322.

importance of making a study of our needs as a race, and applying the remedy accordingly.

Some one may be tempted to ask, Has not the negro boy or girl as good a right to study a French grammar and instrumental music as the white youth? I answer, Yes, but in the present condition of the negro race in this country there is need of something more.

INDUSTRIAL TRAINING NOT THE ONLY EDUCATIONAL SYSTEM FOR NEGROES [5]

Industrial training will be more potent for good to the race when its relation to the other phases of essential education is more clearly understood. There is afloat no end of discussion as to what is the "proper education for the Negro," and much of it is hurtful to the cause it is designed to promote. The danger, at present, that most seriously threatens the success of industrial training, is the ill-advised insistence in certain quarters that this form of education should be offered to the exclusion of all other branches of knowledge. If the idea becomes fixed in the minds of the people that industrial education means class education, that it should be offered to the Negro because he is a Negro, and that the Negro should be confined to this sort of education, then I fear serious injury will be done the cause of hand-training. It should be emphasized that at such institutions as Hampton Institute and Tuskegee Institute, industrial education is not emphasized because colored people are to receive it, but because the ripest educational thought of the world approves it; because the undeveloped material resources of the South make it peculiarly important for both races; and because it should be given in large measure to any race, regardless of color, which is at the same stage of development as the Negro.

On the other hand, no one understanding the real needs of the race would advocate that industrial education should be given to every Negro to the exclusion of the professions and other branches of learning. It is evident that a race so largely segregated as the Negro is, must have an increasing number of its own professional men and women. There is, then, a place and an increasing need for the Negro college as well as for the industrial institute, and the two classes of schools should, and as a matter of fact do, cooperate in the common purpose

[5] Introduction, *Tuskegee and Its People: Their Ideals and Achievements* (New York, 1905), pp. 8–12.

of elevating the masses. There is nothing in hand-training to suggest that it is a class-training. . . .

Tuskegee emphasizes industrial training for the Negro, not with the thought that the Negro should be confined to industrialism, the plow, or the hoe, but because the undeveloped material resources of the South offer at this time a field peculiarly advantageous to the worker skilled in agriculture and the industries, and here are found the Negro's most inviting opportunities for training in the rudimentary elements that ultimately make for a permanently progressive civilization. . . .

As the race gains in knowledge, experience, culture, taste, and wealth, its wants are bound to become more and more diverse; and to satisfy those wants there will be gradually developed within our own ranks— as has already been true of the whites—a constantly increasing variety of professional men and women. . . . There should be no limit placed upon the development of any individual because of color, and let it be understood that no one kind of training can safely be prescribed for any entire race.

4
Economic Foundations for
Attainment of Negro Rights

*Basic to the Washingtonian ideology was the convic-
tion that the progress of the Negro race rests on economic foundations. Instead of fighting a losing battle for political rights Negroes
should work hard, acquire property, and thereby win the respect
of their white neighbors. The conferral of political rights will
follow. To Negroes Washington said that the South offered them
better opportunities for employment and economic progress than
the North. To the white industrialists of the New South he said
that it was to their advantage to employ Negroes, pointing out
that, in contrast to white union labor, Negroes constituted a
reliable, loyal labor force not given to strikes. While stressing
the interdependence of whites and Negroes, he also emphasized
self-help and urged Negroes to establish their own businesses and
become independent of the white community.*

"GREEN POWER" [1]

[In an interview with a newspaper reporter Washington succinctly
stated his thesis, the importance of "green power," and implied that
it was more important than political rights.]

There are reports to the effect that in some sections the black man
has difficulty in voting and having counted the little white ballot
which he has the privilege of depositing about twice every two years,
but there is a little green ballot that he can vote through the teller's
window 313 days in every year and no one will throw it out or refuse
to count it. The man that has the property, the intelligence, the character, is the one that is going to have the largest share in controlling
the government, whether he is white or black, or whether in the North

[1] Indianapolis *Sentinel*, April 23, 1896. Clipping, Booker T. Washington Papers,
Manuscript Division, Library of Congress.

43

or South. It is important that all the privileges of the law be ours;
but it is more important that we be prepared for the exercise of these
privileges.

ECONOMIC PROGRESS OF THE NEGRO LEADS TO
IMPROVED RACE RELATIONS [2]

Nothing else so soon brings about right relations between the two
races in the South as the industrial progress of the negro. Friction between the races will pass away in proportion as the black man, by reason of his skill, intelligence, and character, can produce something that
the white man wants or respects in the commercial world. This is
another reason why at Tuskegee we push the industrial training. We
find that as every year we put into a Southern community colored men
who can start a brickyard, a sawmill, a tin-shop, or a printing-office,—
men who produce something that makes the white man partly dependent upon the negro, instead of all the dependence being on the
other side,—a change takes place in the relations of the races.

Let us go on for a few more years knitting our business and industrial relations into those of the white man, till a black man gets a
mortgage on a white man's house that he can foreclose at will. The
white man on whose house the mortgage rests will not try to prevent
that negro from voting when he goes to the polls. It is through the dairy
farm, the truck garden, the trades, and commercial life, largely, that
the negro is to find his way to the enjoyment of all his rights. Whether
he will or not, a white man respects a negro who owns a two-story
brick house.

THE SOUTH OFFERS THE BEST OPPORTUNITIES
FOR THE NEGRO [3]

Some have advised that the Negro leave the South, and take up his
residence in the Northern states. I question whether this would make
him any better off than he is in the South, when all things are considered. It has been my privilege to study the condition of our people
in nearly every part of America; and I say without hesitation that,

[2] "The Awakening of the Negro," *The Atlantic Monthly*, LXXVIII (September,
1896), 326.
[3] "The Case of the Negro," *The Atlantic Monthly*, LXXXIV (November, 1899),
577, 582, 584.

with some exceptional cases, the Negro is at his best in the Southern states. While he enjoys certain privileges in the North that he does not have in the South, when it comes to the matter of securing property, enjoying business advantages and employment, the South presents a far better opportunity than the North. Few colored men from the South are as yet able to stand up against the severe and increasing competition that exists in the North, to say nothing of the unfriendly influence of labor organizations, which in some way prevents black men in the North, as a rule, from securing occupation in the line of skilled labor.

Another point of great danger for the colored man who goes North is the matter of morals, owing to the numerous temptations by which he finds himself surrounded. More ways offer in which he can spend money than in the South, but fewer avenues of employment for earning money are open to him. . . .

The Negro in the South has it within his power, if he properly utilizes the forces at hand, to make of himself such a valuable factor in the life of the South that for the most part he need not seek privileges, but they will be conferred upon him. To bring this about, the Negro must begin at the bottom and lay a sure foundation, and not be lured by any temptation into trying to rise on a false footing. . . .

The Negro who can make himself so conspicuous as a successful farmer, a large taxpayer, a wise helper of his fellow men, as to be placed in a position of trust and honor by natural selection, whether the position be political or not, is a hundred-fold more secure in that position than one placed there by mere outside force or pressure. I know a Negro, Hon. Isaiah T. Montgomery, in Mississippi, who is mayor of a town; it is true that the town is composed almost wholly of Negroes. Mr. Montgomery is mayor of this town because his genius, thrift, and foresight have created it; and he is held and supported in his office by a charter granted by the state of Mississippi, and by the vote and public sentiment of the community in which he lives. . . .

The Negro should be taught that material development is not an end, but merely a means to an end. . . .

To state in detail just what place the black man will occupy in the South as a citizen, when he has developed in the direction named, is beyond the wisdom of any one. Much will depend upon the sense of justice which can be kept alive in the breast of the American people; almost as much will depend upon the good sense of the Negro himself. That question, I confess, does not give me the most concern just now.

The important and pressing question is, Will the Negro, with his own help and that of his friends, take advantage of the opportunities that surround him? When he has done this, I believe, speaking of his future in general terms, that he will be treated with justice, be given the protection of the law and the recognition which his usefulness and ability warrant. If, fifty years ago, one had predicted that the Negro would receive the recognition and honor which individuals have already received, he would have been laughed at as an idle dreamer. Time, patience, and constant achievement are great factors in the rise of a race.

I do not believe that the world ever takes a race seriously, in its desire to share in the government of a nation, until a large number of individual members of that race have demonstrated beyond question their ability to control and develop their own business enterprises.

LABOR RELATIONS [4]

Custom and contact have so knit the two races together that the black man finds in these Southern states an open sesame in labor, industry, and business that is not surpassed anywhere. It is here alone, by reason of the presence of the Negro, that capital is freed from tyranny and despotism that prevents you from employing whom you please and for that wage that is mutually agreeable and profitable. It is here that that form of slavery which prevents a man from selling his labor to whom he pleases on account of his color is almost unknown. We have had slavery, now dead, that forced an individual to labor without a salary, but none that compelled a man to remain in idleness while his family starved.

The Negro in all parts of the country is beginning to appreciate the advantages which the South affords for earning a living, for commercial development, and in proportion as this is true it will constitute the basis for the settlement of other difficulties. . . . If the black man in the South has a friend in his white neighbor, and a still larger number of friends in his own community, he has a protection and a guarantee of his rights that will be more potent and more lasting than any our Federal Congress or any outside power can confer. While the Negro is grateful for the opportunities which he enjoys in the business of the South, you should remember that you are in debt to the black

[4] Address before the Southern Industrial Convention, Huntsville, Alabama, October 12, 1899, Galveston *News*, October 13, 1899. Clipping, Washington Papers.

man for furnishing you with labor that is almost a stranger to strikes, lock-outs, and labor wars; labor that is law-abiding, peaceful, teachable; labor that is one with you in language, sympathy, religion, and patriotism; labor that has never been tempted to follow the red flag of anarchy, but always the safe flag of his country and the spotless banner of the Cross.

ECONOMIC PROGRESS AS COMPENSATION FOR LOSS OF POLITICAL RIGHTS [5]

When I began my work in Tuskegee in 1881, the colored people of Alabama had just been deprived—in a way that is now familiar—of many of their political rights. There was some voting, but few Negroes held office anywhere in Alabama at that time. The Negroes set great store by the political privileges that had been granted them during the Reconstruction period, and they thought that when they lost these they had lost all. . . .

The people did not say much about their loss. They preserved outwardly, as a rule, the same good nature and cheerfulness which had always characterized them, but deep down in their hearts they had begun to feel that there was no hope for them.

This feeling of apathy and despair continued for a long time among these people in the country districts. A good many of them who owned land in the county at this time gave it up or lost it for one reason or another. Others moved away from the county, and there were a great many abandoned farms. Gradually, however, the temper of the people changed. They began to see that harvests were just as good and just as bad as they had been before the changes which deprived them of their political privileges. They began to see, in short, that there was still hope for them in economic if not in political directions. . . .

A large part of the work which Tuskegee Institute did in those early years, and has continued to do down to the present time, has been to show the masses of our people that in agriculture, in the industries, in commerce, and in the struggle toward economic success, there were compensations for the losses they had suffered in other directions. In doing this we did not seek to give the people the idea that political rights were not valuable or necessary, but rather to impress upon them

[5] "Negro Disfranchisement and the Negro in Business," *The Outlook*, XCIII (October 9, 1909), 310–11, 315. This article was later incorporated into *The Story of the Negro*.

that economic efficiency was the foundation for every kind of success. . . .

The Negro came out of slavery with a feeling that work was the symbol of degradation. In nearly all the schools conducted by Negroes in the South at the present time Negro children are learning to work. The Negro came out of slavery with almost no capital except the hard discipline and training he had received as a slave. In the years since that time he has not only become a large landowner and to a large extent the owner of his own home, but he has become a banker and a business man. He came out of slavery with the idea that somehow or other the Government, which freed him, was going to support and protect him, and that the great hope of his race was in politics and in the ballot. In the last decade the Negro has settled down to the task of building his own fortune and of gaining through thrift, through industry, and through business success that which he has been denied in other directions.

ADVICE TO NEGROES: LAST ADDRESS TO NATIONAL NEGRO BUSINESS LEAGUE [6]

The price of success means beginning at the bottom; it means struggle, it means hardship, it often means hunger, it means planning and sacrificing today that you may possess and enjoy tomorrow; and if you sit idly by and let the other fellow think and plan and lie awake at night, you can rest assured that the other fellow is going to control business everywhere. . . .

Now in the Southland we have about 30,000 Negro business enterprises. We should have within the next few years 20,000 more, and we should not forget or overlook the importance of getting hold of the land, to own a little piece of soil, because a landless race is like a ship without a rudder, and we should get land mighty quick because if those folks in Central Europe ever get through with each other— that is, if any of them are left—they are going to come here by the thousands and by the millions, and we must get our foundation before they come. . . .

Why, don't you know the Greeks have come over here to this coun-

[6] "Last Annual Address as President, delivered before the National Negro Business League, Boston, Mass., August 19, 1915," in *Selected Speeches of Booker T. Washington*, ed. E. Davidson Washington (Garden City, 1932), pp. 262–64, 267. Reprinted by permission of Doubleday & Company, Inc.

try and have taken the shoe-shining trade away from the colored man? Just think of it—the black boy is studying Greek and the Greek boy is blacking shoes! They are becoming independent in this country because they began to lay a foundation for their wealth in the shoe-shining business, and were willing to begin even on a soapbox. They have used that soapbox as a stepping stone to a better business, until they now have well-equipped shoe-shining parlors coupled with hat-cleaning establishments in almost every leading city of our country. Young colored man, you can start in the same humble way right where you are, either in Boston, in New York City, in Montgomery, in New Orleans—start anywhere, and if you will black boots and shoes better than the Greek boy, the white people will come to you, and black people will come to you and help you prosper. . . .

And so, my friends, I hold that there is no hope for us as a race except we learn to apply our education in a practical manner to the resources of our country and to the common activity or the life of the community in which we live. No mere education will help a race except that education be applied to the natural resources and interchange of commodities as represented in such departments of life as farming and business. An ounce of application is worth a ton of abstraction.

5
Race Leader

After his Atlanta Address, delivered in the year of Frederick Douglass's death, Washington was acclaimed the leader of Negro Americans and the successor of Douglass. In the following passage he contrasted his role with that of Douglass. While modestly disclaiming that he had any expectation of achieving his present eminence, he explained how he sought to cultivate the good will and support of three groups who were essential to his success—the white South, the white North, and the members of his own race. Speaking of the power of the Negro press, he denied having any financial interest in any Negro newspaper or having attempted to influence the press financially. He sought to disparage the Negro intellectuals and their criticism of him by suggesting that some of them made a career of exploiting race grievances and asserting that they were too theoretical and had little practical knowledge of southern Negroes and conditions in the South.

DIFFERENT ROLES OF FREDERICK DOUGLASS
AND WASHINGTON [1]

Mr. Douglass's great life-work had been in the political agitation that led to the destruction of slavery. . . . But the long and bitter political struggle in which he had engaged against slavery had not prepared Mr. Douglass to take up the equally difficult task of fitting the Negro for the opportunities and responsibilities of freedom. The same was true to a large extent of other Negro leaders. . . . I felt that the millions of Negroes needed something more than to be reminded of their sufferings and of their political rights; that they needed to do something more than merely to defend themselves.

Frederick Douglass died in February, 1895. In September of the

[1] "Chapters from My Experience," *World's Work*, XXI (November, 1910), 13633–35.

same year I delivered an address in Atlanta at the Cotton States Exposition.

I spoke in Atlanta to an audience composed of leading Southern white people and members of my own race. This seemed to me to be the time and place, without condemning what had been done, to emphasize what ought to be done. I felt that we needed a policy, not of destruction, but of construction; not of defense, but of aggression; a policy, not of hostility or surrender, but of friendship and advance. I stated, as vigorously as I was able, that usefulness in the community where we resided was our surest and most potent protection.

One other point which I made plain in this speech was that, in my opinion, the Negro should seek constantly in very manly, straight forward manner to make friends of the white man by whose side he lived, rather than to content himself with seeking the good-will of some man a thousand miles away. . . .

One of the most surprising results of my Atlanta speech was the number of letters, telegrams, and newspaper editorials that came pouring in upon me from all parts of the country, demanding that I take the place of "leader of the Negro people" left vacant by Frederick Douglass's death, or assuming that I had already taken this place. Until these suggestions began to pour in upon me, I never had the remotest idea that I should be selected or looked upon, in any sense as Frederick Douglass had been, as a leader of the Negro people. I was at that time merely a Negro school-teacher in a rather obscure industrial school.

RELATIONS WITH WHITES—NORTH AND SOUTH [2]

One of the first questions that I had to answer for myself after beginning my work at Tuskegee was how I was to deal with public opinion on the race question. . . .

Of course all these different views about the kind of education that the Negro ought or ought not to have were deeply tinged with racial and sectional feelings. The rule of the "carpet bag" government had just come to an end in Alabama. The masses of the white people were very bitter against the Negroes as a result of the excitement and agitation of the Reconstruction period.

On the other hand, the colored people—who had recently lost, to a very large extent, their place in the politics of the state—were

[2] *Ibid.* (October, 1910), pp. 13505–6, 13509–10, 13520–22.

greatly discouraged and disheartened. Many of them feared they were going to be drawn back into slavery. At this time also there was still a great deal of bitterness between the North and the South in regard to anything that concerned political matters.

I found myself, as it were, at the angle where these opposing forces met. I saw that, in carrying out the work that I had planned, I was likely to be opposed or criticized at some point by each of these parties. On the other hand, I saw just as clearly that in order to succeed I must in some way secure the support and sympathy of each of them. . . .

I knew that Northern people believed, as the South at that time did not believe, in the power of education to inspire, to uplift, and to regenerate the masses of the people. . . . Northern people would be willing and glad to give their support to any school or other agency that proposed to do this in a really fundamental way.

It was, at the same time, plain to me that no effort put forth in behalf of the members of my own race who were in the South was going to succeed unless it finally won the sympathy and support of the best white people in the South. . . .

Finally I had faith in the good common sense of the masses of my own race. . . .

Still it was often a puzzling and a trying problem to determine how best to win and hold the respect of all three of these classes of people, each of which looked with such different eyes and from such widely different points of view at what I was attempting to do.

One thing which gave me faith at the outset and increased my confidence as I went on was the insight which I early gained into the actual relations of the races in the South. I observed, in the first place, that as the result of two hundred and fifty years of slavery the two races had come together in intimate ways that people outside of the South could not understand, and of which the white people and colored people themselves were perhaps not fully conscious. More than that, I perceived that the two races need each other. . . .

Now [since Emancipation] the white man is not only free to assist the Negro in his effort to rise, but he has every motive of self-interest to do so, since to uplift and educate the Negro would reduce the number of paupers and criminals of the race and increase the number of efficiency of its skilled laborers. . . .

As this thought got hold in my mind and I began to see further into the nature of the task that I had undertaken to perform, much of the political agitation and controversy that divided the North from the South, the black man from the white, began to look unreal and artificial to me. It seemed as if the people who carried on political campaigns were engaged to a very large extent in a battle with shadows, and that these shadows represented the prejudices and animosities of a period that was now past. . . .

Many times I have been asked how it is that I have secured the confidence and good wishes of so large a number of white people of the South. My answer in brief is that I have tried to be perfectly frank and straightforward at all times in my relations with them. . . .

I have made it a rule to talk *to* the Southern white people concerning what I might call their shortcomings toward the Negro rather than talk *about* them. In the last analysis, however, I have succeeded in getting the sympathy and support of Southern white people because I have tried to recognize and to face conditions as they actually are, and have honestly tried to work with the best white people in the South to bring about a better condition.

In my own case, I have attempted from the beginning to let every white citizen in my own town see that I am as much interested in the common every-day affairs of life as himself. I tried to let them see that the presence of Tuskegee Institute in the community means better farms and gardens, good housekeeping, good schools, law and order. . . . During all the years that I have lived in Macon County, Ala., I have never had the slightest trouble in either registering or casting my vote at any election. Every white person in the county knows that I am going to vote in a way that will help the county in which I live. . . .

Whatever influence I have gained with the Northern white people has come about from the fact, I think, that they feel that I have tried to use their gifts honestly and in a manner to bring about real and lasting results. I learned long ago that in education as in other things nothing but honest work lasts; fraud and sham are bound to be detected in the end. . . .

Then, in dealing with Northern people, I have always let them know that I did not want to get away from my own race; that I was just as proud of being a Negro as they were of being white people. . . .

The most difficult and trying of the classes of persons with which I am brought in contact is the colored man or woman who is ashamed of his or her color, ashamed of his or her race and, because of this, is always in a bad temper. I have had opportunities, such as few colored men have had, of getting acquainted with many of the best white people, North and South. This has never led me to desire to get away from my own people. On the contrary, I have always returned to my own people and my own work with renewed interest.

RELATIONS WITH THE NEGRO MASSES
AND THE NEGRO PRESS [3]

I determined, that as far as possible, I would try to gain the active support and cooperation, in all that I undertook, of the masses of my own race. . . .

It has always been a great pleasure to me to meet and talk in plain, straight-forward way with the common people of my own race wherever I have been able to meet them. But it is in Negro churches that I have had my best opportunities for meeting and getting acquainted with them. . . .

In carrying out the policy . . . of making use of every opportunity to speak to the masses of the people, I have not only visited country churches, . . . but for years I have made it a practice to attend, whenever it has been possible for me to do so, every important ministers' meeting. I have also made it a practice to visit town and city churches and in this way to get acquainted with the ministers and meet the people.

During my many and long campaigns in the North, for the purpose of getting money to carry on Tuskegee Institute, it has been a great pleasure and satisfaction to me, after I had spoken in some white church or hall or at some banquet, to go directly to some colored church for a heart-to-heart talk with my own people. . . .

This does not mean that colored people may not attend the other meetings which I address, but means simply that they prefer in most cases to have me speak to them alone. . . .

Next to the church, I think it is safe to say that the secret societies or beneficial orders bring together greater numbers of colored people and exercise a larger influence upon the race than any other kind of organization. . . .

Another agency which exercises tremendous power among Negroes

[3] *Ibid.*, pp. 13516–19. Washington is less than candid in speaking of his relations with the Negro press. In reality he was for a time part-owner of the New York *Age* and subsidized in one way or another a large number of Negro publications.

is the Negro press. Few if any persons outside the Negro race understand the power and influence of the Negro newspaper. In all, there are about two hundred newspapers published by colored men at different points in the United States. . . . With the exception of about three, these two hundred newspapers have stood loyally by me in all my plans and policies to uplift the race. I have called upon them freely to aid me in making known my plans and ideas, and they have always responded in a most generous fashion to all the demands that I have made upon them.

It has been suggested to me at different times that I should purchase a Negro newspaper in order that I might have an "organ" to make known my views on matters concerning the policies and interests of the race. Certain persons have suggested also that I pay money to certain of these papers in order to make sure that they support my views.

I confess that there have frequently been times when it seemed that the easiest way to combat some statement that I knew to be false or to correct some impression which seemed to me peculiarly injurious, would be to have a paper of my own or to pay for the privilege of setting forth my own views in the editorial columns of some paper which I did not own.

I am convinced, however, that either of these two courses would have proved fatal. The minute that it should become known—and it would be known—that I owned an "organ," the other papers would cease to support me as they now do. If I should attempt to use money with some papers, I should soon have to use it with all. If I should pay for the support of newspapers once, I should have to go on paying all the time. Very soon I should have around me, if I should succeed in bribing them, a lot of hired men and no sincere and earnest supporters. Although I might gain for myself some apparent and temporary advantage in this way, I should destroy the value and influence of the very papers that support me.

NEGRO INTELLECTUALS [4]

My determination to stand by the programme which I had worked out during the years I had been at Tuskegee and which I had expressed in my Atlanta speech, soon brought me into conflict with a small group who styled themselves "The Intellectuals," at other

[4] *Ibid.* (November, 1910), pp. 13637–38, 13640.

times "The Talented Tenth." As most of these men were graduates of Northern colleges and made their homes for the most part in the North, it was natural enough, I suppose, that they should feel that leadership in all race matters should remain, as heretofore, in the North. At any rate, they were opposed to any change from the policy of uncompromising and relentless antagonism to the South so long as there seemed to them to be anything in Southern conditions wrong or unjust to the Negro. . . .

The first thing to which they objected was my plan for the industrial education of the Negro. It seemed to them that in teaching colored people to work with the hands I was making too great a concession to public opinion in the South. . . .

According to their way of looking at the matter, the Southern white man was the natural enemy of the Negro, and any attempt, no matter for what purpose, to gain his sympathy or support must be regarded as a kind of treason to the race.

All these matters furnished fruitful subjects for controversy, in all of which the college graduates that I have referred to were naturally the leaders. . . .

I remember one young man in particular who graduated from Yale University and afterward took a post-graduate course at Harvard, and who began his career by delivering a series of lectures on "The Mistakes of Booker T. Washington." It was not long, however, before he found that he could not live continuously on my mistakes. Then he discovered that in all his schooling he had not fitted himself to perform any kind of useful and productive labor. After he had failed in several other directions he appealed to me, and I tried to find something for him to do. It is pretty hard, however, to help a young man who has started wrong. Once he gets the idea that—because he had crammed his head full with mere book knowledge —the world owes him a living it is hard for him to change. The last time I heard of the young man in question, he was trying to eke out a miserable existence as a book-agent while he was looking about for a position somewhere with the Government as a janitor or for some other equally humble occupation. . . .

Among the most trying class of people with whom I come in contact are the persons who have been educated in books to the extent that they are able, upon every occasion, to quote a phrase or a sentiment from Shakespeare, Milton, Cicero, or some other great writer. Every time any problem arises they are on the spot with a phrase or a quotation. . . .

In college they studied problems and solved them on paper. But these problems had already been solved by some one else, and all that they had to do was to learn the answers. They had never faced any unsolved problems in college, and all that they learned had not taught them the patience and persistence which alone solve real problems. . . .

There is another class of colored people who make a business of keeping the troubles, the wrongs, and the hardships of the Negro race before the public. Having learned that they are able to make a living out of their troubles, they have grown into the settled habit of advertising their wrongs—partly because they want sympathy and partly because it pays.

Some of these people do not want the Negro to lose his grievances because they do not want to lose their jobs. . . .

My experience is that people who call themselves "The Intellectuals" understand theories but they do not understand things. I have long been convinced that, if these men had gone into the South and taken up and become interested in some practical work which would have brought them in touch with people and things, the whole world would have looked very different to them. Bad as conditions might have seemed at first, when they saw that actual progress was being made, they would have taken a more hopeful view of the situation. . . .

The truth is, I suspect, as I have already suggested, that "The Intellectuals" live too much in the past. They know books but they do not know men. They know a great deal about the slavery controversy, for example, but they know almost nothing about the Negro. Especially are they ignorant in regard to the actual needs of the colored people in the South today.

6
Relations Between Negroes and Whites

A belief in the interdependence and mutual interests of Negroes and whites is the foundation for the system of race relations which Washington envisioned. He frequently asserted, as in the first selection below, that he had risen above any feeling of bitterness toward the white race. He felt that improved race relations in the South would come from within as Negroes improved their economic condition, but civil rights laws imposed by the federal government he considered futile. While stressing mutuality of interests, in the article "The Negro's Place in American Life," he sought to show white Americans the lengths to which the Negro was forced to go to "keep in his place" and to avoid crossing "the color line," which white society had drawn. But, after mentioning the furor created when he dined at the White House, he said that in the matter of social relations it was best to respect local customs, and that he did not quarrel with the customs of the South (i.e., segregation). In the last selection, an address which he delivered to an all-Negro audience at the national convention of the Afro-American Council, he emphasized the duties and responsibilities of Negroes in the field of race relations. He advised them to exercise self-control, to be law-abiding, to avoid extremism, and to concentrate on constructive achievement instead of complaining about the wrongs they suffer.

RACE PREJUDICE IS DEGRADING [1]

I learned the lesson that great men cultivate love, and that only little men cherish a spirit of hatred. I learned that assistance given to the weak makes the one who gives it strong; and that oppression of the unfortunate makes one weak.

It is now long ago that I learned this lesson . . . and resolved

[1] *Up From Slavery: An Autobiography* (New York, 1901), p. 165.

that I would permit no man, no matter what his colour might be, to narrow and degrade my soul by making me hate him. With God's help, I believe that I have completely rid myself of any ill feeling toward the Southern white man for any wrong that he may have inflicted upon my race. I am made to feel just as happy now when I am rendering service to Southern white men as when the service is rendered to a member of my own race. I pity from the bottom of my heart any individual who is so unfortunate as to get into the habit of holding race prejudice.

RACIAL PROBLEMS NOT SOLVED BY CIVIL RIGHTS LAWS [2]

Any movement for the elevation of the Southern Negro, in order to be successful, must have to a certain extent the cooperation of the Southern whites. They control government and own the property—whatever benefits the black man benefits the white man. The proper education of all the whites will benefit the Negro as much as the education of the Negro will benefit the whites. The Governor of Alabama would probably count it no disgrace to ride in the same railroad coach with a colored man, but the ignorant white man who curries the Governor's horse would turn up his nose in disgust. . . .

Brains, property, and character for the Negro will settle the question of civil rights. The best course to pursue in regard to the civil rights bill in the South is to let it alone; let it alone and it will settle itself. Good teachers and plenty of money to pay them will be more potent in settling the race question than many civil rights bills and investigating committees. . . . Let there be in a community a Negro who by virtue of his superior knowledge of the chemistry of the soils, his acquaintance with the most improved tools and best breeds of stock, can raise fifty bushels of corn to the acre while his white neighbor only raises thirty, and the white man will come to the black man to learn. Further, they will sit down in the same train, in the same coach and on the same seat to talk about it. Harmony will come in proportion as the black man gets something that the white man wants, whether it be of brains or material. . . .

My faith is that reforms in the South are to come from within.

[2] "The Educational Outlook in the South," *Journals of the Proceedings and Addresses of the National Educational Association, Session of the Year, 1884, at Madison, Wisconsin* (Boston, 1885), pp. 126–28.

Southern people have a good deal of human nature. They like to receive the praise of doing good deeds, and they don't like to obey orders that come from Washington telling them that they must lay aside at once customs that they have followed for centuries, and henceforth there must be but one railroad coach, one hotel, and one schoolhouse for ex-master and ex-slave. . . .

Now, in regard to what I have said about the relations of the two races, there should be no unmanly cowering or stooping to satisfy unreasonable whims of Southern white men, but it is charity and wisdom to keep in mind the two hundred years' schooling in prejudice against the Negro which the ex-slaveholders are called upon to conquer.

"THE NEGRO'S PLACE IN AMERICAN LIFE" [3]

One of the most striking and interesting things about the American Negro, and one which has impressed itself upon my mind more and more . . . is the extent to which the black man has intertwined his life with that of the people of the white race about him. While it is true that hardly any other race of people that has come to this country has remained in certain respects so separate and distinct a part of the population as the Negro, it is also true that no race that has come to this country has so woven its life into the life of the people about it. No race has shared to a greater extent in the work and activities of the original settlers of the country, or has been more closely related to them in interest, in sympathy, and in sentiment than the Negro race.

In fact, there is scarcely any enterprise of any moment that has been undertaken by a member of the white race in which the Negro has not had some part. In all the great pioneer work of clearing forests and preparing the way for civilization the Negro, as I have tried to point out, has had his part. In all the difficult and dangerous work of exploration of the country the Negro has invariably been the faithful companion and helper of the white man. . . .

I have described the manner in which the Negro has adapted his own life to that of the people around him, uniting his interests and his sympathies with those of the dominant white race. Perhaps I should say a word here of the way in which he has managed to keep

[3] "The Negro's Place in American Life," *The Outlook*, XCIII (November 13, 1909), 579, 582–84. This article was a part of *The Story of the Negro*.

his life separate and to prevent friction in his dealings with the other portions of the community. Few white people, I dare say, realize what the Negro has to do, to what extent he has been compelled to go out of his way, to avoid causing trouble and prevent friction.

For example, in one large city, I know of a business place in which there is a cigar-stand, a bootblacking-stand, a place for cleaning hats, and a barber shop, all in one large room. Any Negro can, without question, have his hat cleaned, his boots blacked, or buy a cigar in this place, but he cannot take a seat in the barber's chair. The minute he should do this he would be asked to go somewhere else.

The Negro must, at all hazard and in all times and places, avoid crossing the color line. It is a little difficult, however, sometimes to determine upon what principle this line is drawn. For instance, customs differ in different parts of the same town, as well as in different parts of the country at large. In one part of a town a Negro may be able to get a meal at a public lunch-counter, but in another part of the same town he cannot do so. . . .

In all these different situations, somehow or other, the Negro manages to comport himself so as rarely to excite comment or cause trouble.

He often hears the opinion expressed that the Negro should keep his place or that he is "all right in his place." People who make use of these expressions seldom understand how difficult it is, considering the different customs in different parts of the country, to find out just what his place is. . . .

As illustrating the ability of the Negro to avoid the rocks and shoals which he is likely to meet in traveling about the country and still manage to get what he wants, I recall an experience of a colored man with whom I was traveling through South Carolina some time ago. This man was very anxious to reach the railway train, and had only a few minutes in which to do so. He hailed, naturally enough, the first hackman he saw, who happened to be a white man. The white man told him that it was not his custom to carry Negroes in his carriage. The colored man, not in the least disturbed, at once replied: "That's all right, we will fix that; you get in the carriage and I'll take the front seat and drive you." This was done, and in a few minutes they reached the depot, in time to catch the train. The colored man handed the white man twenty-five cents and departed. Both were satisfied, and the color line was preserved. . . .

In living in the midst of seventy millions of the most highly

civilized people of the world the Negro has the opportunity to learn much that he could not learn in a community where the people were less enlightened and less progressive. On the other hand, it is a disadvantage to him that his progress is constantly compared to the progress of a people who have the advantage of many centuries of civilization, while the Negro has for only a little more than forty years been a free man. If the American Negro, with his present degree of advancement, were living in the midst of a civilization such as exists to-day in Asia or in the south of Europe, the gap between him and the people by whom he is surrounded would not then be so wide, and he would receive credit for the progress that he has already made. . . .

The story of the American Negro has been one of progress from the first. While there have been times when it seemed the race was going backward, this backward movement has been temporal, local, or merely apparent. On the whole, the Negro has been and is moving forward everywhere and in every direction. . . .

The story of the Negro, in the last analysis, is simply the story of the man who is farthest down; as he raises himself he raises every other man who is above him. . . .

To me the history of the Negro people in America seems like the story of a great adventure in which, for my own part, I am glad to have had a share. So far from being a misfortune, it seems to me that it is a rare privilege to have part in the struggles, the plans, and the ambitions of ten millions of people who are making their way from slavery to freedom.

THE WHITE HOUSE DINNER—SOCIAL RELATIONS BETWEEN THE RACES [4]

This trip to Washington brings me to a matter which I have hitherto constantly refused to discuss in print or in public, though I have had a great many requests to do so. At the time, I did not care to add fuel to the controversy which it aroused, and I speak of it now only because it seems to me that an explanation will show the incident in its true light and in its proper proportions.

When I reached Mr. [Whitefield] McKinlay's house, I found an in-

[4] "Chapters from My Experience," *World's Work*, XXI (February, 1911), 14037–39.

vitation from President Roosevelt, asking me to dine with him at the White House that evening at eight o'clock. At the hour appointed I went to the White House and dined with the President and members of his family and a gentleman from Colorado. After dinner we talked at considerable length concerning plans about the South which the President had in mind. . . .

Some newspapers attempted to weave into this incident a deliberate and well-planned scheme on the part of President Roosevelt to lead the way in bringing about the social intermingling of the two races. I am sure that nothing was farther from the President's mind than this; certainly it was not in my mind. Mr. Roosevelt simply found that he could spare the time best during and after the dinner-hour for the discussion of the matters which both of us were interested in.

The public interest aroused by this dinner seemed all the more extraordinary and uncalled for because, on previous occasions, I had taken tea with Queen Victoria at Windsor Castle; I had dined with the Governors of nearly every state in the North; I had dined in the same room with President McKinley at Chicago at the Peace-Jubilee dinner; and I had dined with ex-President Harrison in Paris, and with many other prominent men. . . .

I have come to the conclusion that prejudices are something that it does not pay to disturb. It is best to "let sleeping dogs lie." All sections of the United States, like all other parts of the world, have their own peculiar customs and prejudices. Where these customs have grown up slowly and become firmly established, it will generally be found that they are there because they serve some good purpose—or have done so in the past. For that reason it is the part of common sense to respect them. . . . In the South, it is not the custom for colored and white people to be entertained at the same hotel; it is not the custom for black and white children to attend the same school. In most parts of the North a different custom prevails. I have never stopped to question or quarrel with the customs of the people in the part of the country in which I found myself. . . .

I was born in the South and I understand thoroughly the prejudices, the customs, the traditions of the South—and, strange as it may seem to those who do not wholly understand the situation, I love the South. There is no Southern white man who cherishes a deeper interest than I in everything that promotes the progress and glory of the South. For that reason, if for no other, I will never willingly and knowingly do anything that in my opinion will provoke bitterness between the races or misunderstanding between the North and the South.

THE RESPONSIBILITIES OF THE NEGRO [5]

Whatever progress is made in the years that are to come will result largely from open, frank discussion and a sympathetic cooperation between the highest types of whites and the same class of blacks. One thing of which I feel absolutely sure is that without mutual confidence and cooperation there is little hope for the progress which we all desire. In the present season of anxiety, and almost of despair, which possesses an element of the race, there are two things which I will say as strongly as I may.

First, let no man of the race become discouraged or hopeless. Though their voices may not be often or loudly lifted, there are in this country, North and South, men who mean to help see that justice is meted out to the race in all avenues of life. . . . There is a class of brave, earnest men in the South, as well as in the North, who are more determined than ever before to see that the race is given an opportunity to elevate itself; and we owe it to these friends as well as to ourselves to see that no act of ours causes them embarrassment.

Second, let us keep before us the fact that, almost without exception, every race or nation that has ever got upon its feet has done so through struggle and trial and persecution; and that out of this very resistance to wrong, out of the struggle against odds, it has gained strength, self-confidence, and experience which it could not have gained in any other way.

And not the least of the blessings of such struggle is that it keeps one humble and nearer to the heart of the Giver of all gifts. Show me the individual who is permitted to go through life without anxious thought, without ever having experienced a sense of poverty and wrong, want and struggle, and I will show you a man who is likely to fail in life. "Whom the Lord loveth, He chasteneth." . . .

During the season through which we are now passing, I wish to ask, with all the emphasis I am able to command, that each individual of the race keep a calm mind and exercise the greatest self-control; and that we all keep a brave heart. Let nothing lead us into extremes

[5] Address before Afro-American Council in Louisville, July 3, 1903 in Topeka. Kansas, *Capital,* July 19, 1903. Clipping, Washington Papers.

of utterance or action. By this method of procedure we shall be able to justify the faith of our friends and confound our enemies. In the affairs of a race, as with great business enterprises, it is the individual of few words and conservative action who commands respect and confidence. Vastly more courage is often shown in one's ability to suffer in silence, or to keep the body under control when sorely tempted, than in acting through the medium of a mob. . . .

In advocating this policy I am not asking that the Negro act the coward; we are not cowards. The part which we have played in defending the flag of our country in every war in which we have been engaged is sufficient evidence of our courage when the proper time comes to manifest it.

The recent outbreaks of government by the mob emphasize two lessons, one for our race and one for the other citizens of our country, South and North; for it is to be noted, I repeat, that the work of the lyncher is not confined to one section of the country.

The lesson for us is that we should see to it that so far as the influence of parent, of school, of pulpit, and of press is concerned, no effort be spared to impress upon our own people, especially the youth, that idleness and crime should cease, and that no excuse be given the world to label any large proportion of the race as idlers and criminals; and that we show ourselves as anxious as any other class of citizens to bring to punishment those who commit crime, when proper legal procedure is sure. We should let the world know on all proper occasions that we consider no legal punishment too severe for the wretch of any race who attempts to outrage a woman.

The lesson for the other portion of the nation to learn is that, both in the making and the execution, the same laws should be made to apply to the Negro as to the white man. There should be meted out equal justice to the black man and the white man whether it relates to citizenship, the protection of property, the right to labor, or the protection of human life. Whenever the nation forgets, or is tempted to forget, this basic principle, the whole fabric of government for both the white and the black man is weakened and threatened with destruction. . . .

In our efforts to go forward, . . . we should bear in mind that our ability and our progress will be measured largely by evidences of tangible, visible worth. We have a right in a conservative and sensible manner to enter our complaints, but we shall make a fatal error if we yield to the temptation of believing that mere opposition to our wrongs, and the simple utterance of complaint, will take the place of progressive, constructive action, which must constitute the bedrock of all true civilization. The weakest race or individual can condemn a policy; it is the work of a statesman to construct one. A race is not measured by its ability to condemn, but to create. Let us hold up our heads and with firm and steady tread go manfully forward. No one likes to feel that he is continually following a funeral procession. . . .

The whites and the blacks are to reside together in this country permanently, and we should lose no opportunity to cultivate in every straightforward, manly way the greatest harmony between the races. Whoever, North or South, black or white, by word or deed needlessly stirs up strife is an enemy to both races and to his country.

7
Politics and Suffrage

*Washington's statements on political rights and polit-
ical activities of Negroes were somewhat ambiguous, but his tone
was frequently deprecatory. In the appeal to the Louisiana Constitutional Convention below he took the position that the South
was justified in imposing educational and property requirements
for voting but that tests should apply to both races equally, a
position which he frequently reiterated in later writings. In the
other selections he expressed the opinion that for the time being
Negroes should be modest in claiming and exercising political
rights, but as they acquired property and respectability opposition
to their political activity would decline since they would be regarded as "safe" voters. As for himself—he stated that he never
liked politics and never had political ambitions, but he admitted
that President Theodore Roosevelt consulted him on political
questions and that during the Roosevelt administration he played
some part in politics.*

APPEAL TO THE LOUISIANA CONSTITUTIONAL
CONVENTION [1]

To the Louisiana State Constitutional Convention . . .

I am no politician; on the other hand, I have always advised my
race to give attention to acquiring property, intelligence and character
as the necessary bases of good citizenship, rather than to mere political
agitation. But the question upon which I write is out of the region of
ordinary politics; it affects the civilization of two races, not for to-day
alone but for a very long time to come: it is up in the region of duty
of man to man, of Christian to Christian. . . .

The negro agrees with you that it is necessary to the salvation of
the south that restriction be put upon the ballot. I know that you
have two serious problems before you; ignorant and corrupt government on the one hand, and on the other a way to restrict the ballot so
that control will be in the hands of the intelligent without regard to

[1] New Orleans *Daily Picayune,* February 21, 1898.

race. With the sincerest sympathy with you in your efforts to find a way out of the difficulty, I want to suggest that no state in the south can make a law that will provide an opportunity or temptation for an ignorant white man to vote and withhold the same opportunity from an ignorant colored man, without injuring both men. . . .

The negro does not object to an educational or property test, but let the law be so clear that no one clothed with state authority will be tempted to perjure and degrade himself, by putting one interpretation upon it for the white man and another for the black man. Study the history of the south, and you will find that where there has been the most dishonesty in the matter of voting, there you will find to-day the lowest moral condition of both races. . . .

I beg of you, further, that in the degree that you close the ballot box against the ignorant that you open the school house. More than one-half of the people of your state are negroes. No state can long prosper when a large percentage of its citizenship is in ignorance and poverty and has no interest in government. I beg of you that you do not treat us as an alien people. We are not aliens. You know us; you know that we have cleared your forests, tilled your fields, nursed your children and protected your families. There is an attachment between us that few understand. While I do not presume to be able to advise you, yet it is in my heart to say that if your convention would do something that would prevent, for all time, strained relations between the two races, and would permanently settle the matter of political relations in one southern state at least, let the very best educational opportunities be provided for both races: and added to this the enactment of an election law that shall be incapable of unjust discrimination, at the same time providing that in proportion as the ignorant secure education, property and character, they will be given all the rights of citizenship. Any other course will take from one-half your citizens interest in the state and hope and ambition to become intelligent producers and taxpayers—to become useful and virtuous citizens.

HOW THE NEGRO WILL ATTAIN POLITICAL RIGHTS [2]

My own belief is, although I have never before said so in so many words, that the time will come when the Negro in the South will be accorded all the political rights which his ability, character, and

[2] *Up From Slavery: An Autobiography* (New York, 1901), pp. 234-37.

material possessions entitle him to. I think, though, that the opportunity to freely exercise such political rights will not come in any
large degree through outside or artificial forcing, but will be accorded
to the Negro by the Southern white people themselves, and that they
will protect him in the exercise of those rights. . . .

I believe it is the duty of the Negro—as the greater part of the
race is already doing—to deport himself modestly in regard to
political claims, depending upon the slow but sure influences that
proceed from the possession of property, intelligence, and high character for the full recognition of his political rights. I think that the
according of the full exercise of political rights is going to be a
matter of natural, slow growth, not an over-night, gourd-vine affair.
I do not believe that the Negro should cease voting, for a man cannot
learn the exercise of self-government by ceasing to vote any more
than a boy can learn to swim by keeping out of the water, but I do
believe that in his voting he should more and more be influenced
by those of intelligence and character who are his next-door neigh-
bours. . . .

I do not believe that any state should make a law that permits an
ignorant and poverty-stricken white man to vote, and prevents a
black man in the same condition from voting. . . .

As a rule, I believe in universal, free suffrage, but I believe that
in the South we are confronted with peculiar conditions that justify
the protection of the ballot in many of the states, for a while at
least, either by an educational test, a property test, or by both
combined; but whatever tests are required, they should be made to
apply with equal and exact justice to both races.

PROPERTIED NEGROES ARE "SAFE" VOTERS [3]

[White citizens of the South realized that] when a Negro became
the owner of a home and was a taxpayer, having a regular trade
or other occupation, he at once became a conservative and safe citizen
and voter; one who would consider the interests of the whole community before casting his ballot; and, further, one whose ballot could
not be purchased.

One case in point is that of the twenty-eight teachers at our school
in Tuskegee who applied for life-voting certificates under the new

[3] 'Fruits of Industrial Training," *The Atlantic Monthly*, XCII (October, 1903),
460.

constitution of Alabama, not one was refused registration; and if I may be forgiven a personal reference, in my case, the Board of Registers were kind enough to send me special request to the effect that they wished me not to fail to register as a life voter. I do not wish to convey the impression that all worthy colored people have been registered in Alabama, because there have been many inexcusable and unlawful omissions; but, with few exceptions, the 2700 who have been registered represent the best Negroes in the state.

PROPERTIED NEGROES EXERT INFLUENCE
WITHOUT THE VOTE [4]

In regard to the political influence of the Negro, I might say, also, that close observation in every State in the South convinces me that while the Negro does not go through the form of casting the ballot in order to express his political influence to the extent that the white man does, in every Southern community there is a group of property-holding men, and often women, of high character, who do always exert political influence in the matters that concern the protection and progress of their race. Sometimes this influence is exerted individually, sometimes in a group, but it is felt nevertheless. I know any number of Negroes in the South whose influence is so strong because of their character that their wish or word expressed to a local or State official will go almost as far as the word of any white man will go. There is a kind of influence that the man exerts who is prosperous, intelligent, and possesses high character, a kind of influence that is intangible and hard to define, but which no law can deprive him of.

I do not mean to suggest that the sort of personal influence I have described is in any way a substitute for the ballot, or can be expected to take its place. It ought to be clearly recognized that, in a republican form of government, if any group of people is left permanently without the franchise they are placed at a serious disadvantage.

WASHINGTON'S PERSONAL ATTITUDE TOWARD POLITICS—
RELATIONS WITH THEODORE ROOSEVELT [5]

Some years ago—and not so very many, either—I think that I should be perfectly safe in saying that the highest ambition of the

---

[4] "Law and Order and the Negro," *The Outlook*, XCIII (November 6, 1909), 551. This article was incorporated into *The Story of the Negro*.

[5] "Chapters from My Experience," *World's Work*, XXI (February, 1911), 14032, 14034–35, 14037.

average Negro in America was to hold some sort of office, or to have some sort of job that connected him with the Government. . . .

I do not think that I ever shared that feeling of so many others of my race. . . . I early saw that it was impossible to build up a race of which the leaders were spending most of their time, thought, and energy in trying to get into office, or in trying to stay there after they were in. . . .

I do not like politics, and yet, in recent years, I have had some experience in political matters. However, no man who is interested in public questions of any kind can ever entirely escape having something to do with politics, no matter how slight or by what name it is called. And, in fact, it was just because it was well-known that I seek no political office outside of an honorary one, that such connection as I have had with politics came about. . . .

Let me add that I have known many public men and have studied them carefully, but the best and highest example of a man that was the same in political office that he was in private life is Colonel Theodore Roosevelt. . . .

I was thrown, comparatively early in my career, into contact with Colonel Roosevelt. He was just the sort of man of whom any one who was trying to do work of any kind for the improvement of any race or type of humanity would naturally go to for advice and help. . . . In fact, I have no hesitation in saying that I consider him the highest type of all-round man that I have ever met. . . .

I question whether any man ever went into the Presidency with a more sincere desire to be of real service to the South than Mr. Roosevelt did. . . .

During the fall of 1901, while I was making a tour of Mississippi, I received word to the effect that the President would like to have a conference with me, as soon as it was convenient, concerning some important matters. With a friend, who was traveling with me, I discussed very seriously the question whether, with the responsibilities I already had, I should take on others. After considering the matter carefully, we decided that the only policy to pursue was to face the new responsibilities as they arose, because new responsibilities bring new opportunities for usefulness of which I ought to take advantage in the interest of my race. I was the more disposed to feel that this was a duty, because Mr. Roosevelt was proposing to carry out the very policies which I had advocated ever since I began work in Alabama.

8
Washington Protests Against
Racial Injustice

Washington was invariably restrained in his criticism of the injustices and outrages perpetrated against members of his race. In the first selection below he implied that Negroes are by nature long-suffering and unresentful.

He was more outspoken in his condemnation of lynching than of any other form of injustice against Negroes. In a letter to the press which was widely publicized he pointed out the increase in the number and brutality of lynchings. Such barbarities, he said, are inexcusable in a society which claims to be influenced by the precepts of Christianity. In the final selection, "Is the Negro Having a Fair Chance?" his language is still guarded, but the article illustrates a tendency in his later years to be somewhat more explicit than in his earlier writings in pointing out the grievances which Negroes suffered in the South.

LYNCHING

In an interview Washington was asked whether lynching had stirred up Negroes to the point that there was danger of race war or insurrection. He replied:

No, not at all. God did not put very much combativeness into our race. Perhaps it would have been better for us if we had not gone on licking the hand that had beaten us. But that is the way of our race.[1]

The following appeal written by Washington was published in newspapers throughout the United States.

Within the last fortnight three members of my race have been burned at the stake; of these one was a woman. Not one of the

[1] Minneapolis *Journal,* February 2, 1896. Clipping, Washington Papers.

three was charged with any crime even remotely connected with the abuse of a white woman. In every case murder was the sole accusation. All of these burnings took place in broad daylight and two of them occurred on Sunday afternoon in sight of a Christian church.

In the midst of the nation's busy and prosperous life few, I fear, take time to consider where these brutal and inhuman practices are leading us. The custom of burning human beings has become so common as scarcely to excite interest or attract unusual attention.

I have always been among those who condemned in the strongest terms crimes of whatever character committed by members of my race, and I condemn them now with equal severity; but I maintain that the only protection of our civilization is a fair and calm trial of all the people charged with crime and in their legal punishment if proved guilty.

There is no shadow of excuse of departure from legal methods in the cases of individuals accused of murder. The laws are as a rule made by the white people and their execution is in the hands of the white people; so that there is little probability of any guilty colored man escaping.

These burnings without trial are in the deepest sense unjust to my race; but it is not this injustice alone which stirs my heart. These barbarous scenes followed, as they are, by the publication of the shocking details are more disgraceful and degrading to the people who inflict the punishment than those who receive it.

If the law is disregarded when a negro is concerned, it will soon be disregarded when a white man is concerned. . . .

Worst of all these outrages take place in communities where there are Christian churches; in the midst of people who have their Sunday schools, their Christian Endeavor societies and Young Men's Christian Association, where collections are taken up for sending missionaries to Africa and China and the rest of the so-called heathen world.

Is it not possible for pulpit and press to speak out against these burnings in a manner that shall arouse a public sentiment that will compel the mob to cease insulting our courts, our Governors and our legal authority; cease bringing shame and ridicule upon our Christian civilization? [2]

[2] *Montgomery Advertiser*, February 29, 1905. Clipping, Washington Papers.

IS THE NEGRO HAVING A FAIR CHANCE? [3]

The uncertainty, the constant fear and expectation of rebuff which the colored man experiences in the North, is often more humiliating and more wearing than the frank and impersonal discrimination which he meets in the South. This is all the more true because the colored youth in most of the Northern States, educated as they are in the same schools with white youths, taught by the same teachers, and inspired by the same ideals of American citizenship, are not prepared for the discrimination that meets them when they leave school.

Despite all this, it cannot be denied that the negro has advantages in the North which are denied him in the South. They are the opportunity to vote and to take part, to some extent, in making and administering the laws by which he is governed, the opportunity to obtain an education, and, what is of still greater importance, fair and unbiased treatment in the courts, the protection of the law.

I have touched upon conditions North and South, which, whether they affect the negro favorably or adversely, are for the most part so firmly entrenched in custom, prejudice, and human nature that they must perhaps be left to the slow changes of time. There are certain conditions in the South, however, in regard to which colored people feel perhaps more keenly because they believe if they were generally understood they would be remedied. Very frequently the negro people suffer injury and wrong in the South because they have or believe they have no way of making their grievances known. Not only are they not represented in the legislatures, but it is sometimes hard to get a hearing even in the press. . . .

One thing that many negroes feel keenly, although they do not say much about it to either black or white people, is the conditions of railway travel in the South.

Now and then the negro is compelled to travel. With few exceptions, the railroads are almost the only great business concerns in the South that pursue the policy of taking just as much money from the black

[3] "Is the Negro Having a Fair Chance?" *Century*, LXXIV (November, 1912), 51–55. Other articles written in the closing years of his life more openly critical of injustice and discrimination and less conciliatory in tone than most of Washington's writings were: "Black and White in the South: Schools for Negroes," *The Outlook*, CVI (March 14, 1914), 590–93; and "My View of Segregation Laws," *New Republic*, V (December 4, 1915), 113–14.

traveler as from the white traveler without feeling that they ought, as a matter of justice and fair play, not as a matter of social equality, to give one man for his money just as much as another man. The failure of most of the roads to do justice to the negro when he travels is the source of more bitterness than any one other matter of which I have any knowledge.

What embitters the colored people in regard to railroad travel, I repeat, is not the separation but the inadequacy of the accommodations. . . .

In the matter of education, the negro in the South has not had what Colonel Roosevelt calls a "square deal." . . .

It is only natural that the negro in the South should feel that he is unfairly treated when he has, as is often true in the country districts, either no school at all or one with a term of no more than four or five months, taught in the wreck of a log-cabin and by a teacher who is paid about half of the price of a first-class convict.

This is no mere rhetorical statement. If a negro steals or commits a murderous assault of some kind, he will be tried and imprisoned, and then, if he is classed as a first-class convict, he will be rented out at the rate of $46 per month for twelve months in the year. The negro who does not commit a crime, but prepares himself to serve the State as a first-grade teacher, will receive from the State for that service perhaps $30 per month for a period of not more than six months.

Taking the Southern States as a whole, about $10.23 per capita is spent in educating the average white boy or girl, and the sum of $2.82 per capita in educating the average black child. . . .

Every one agrees that a public library in a city tends to make better citizens, keeping people usefully employed instead of spending their time in idleness or committing crime. Is it fair, as is true in most of the large cities of the South, to take the negro's money in the form of taxes to support a public library, and then to make no provisions for the negro using any library? . . .

It would help mightily toward the higher civilization of both races if more white people would apply their religion to the negro in their community, and ask themselves how they would like to be treated if they were in the negro's place. For example, no white man in America would feel that he was being treated with justice if every time he had a case in court, whether civil or criminal, every member of the jury was of some other race. Yet this is true of the negro in nearly all of the Southern States. There are few white lawyers or judges who will not admit privately that it is almost impossible for a negro to get justice when he has a case against a white man and all the members of the jury are white. In these circumstances when a negro fails to receive justice, the injury to him is temporary, but the injury to the character of the white man on the jury is permanent.

In Alabama eighty-five per cent of the convicts are negroes. The official records show that last year Alabama had turned into its treasury $1,085,854 from the labor of convicts. At least $900,000 of this came from negro convicts, who were for the most part rented to the coal-mining companies in the northern part of the State. The result of this policy has been to get as many able-bodied convicts as possible into the mines, so that contractors might increase their profits. . . . The point is . . . that while $900,000 is turned into the state treasury from negro-convict labor, to say nothing of negro taxes, there came out of the State treasury, to pay negro teachers only $357,585. . . .

In most Southern States it is absolutely necessary that some restriction be placed upon the use of the ballot. The actual methods by which this restriction was brought about have been widely advertised, and there is no necessity for me discussing them here. At the time these measures were passed I urged that, whatever law went upon the statute-book in regard to the use of the ballot, it should apply with absolute impartiality to both races. This policy I advocate again in justice to both white man and negro. . . .

I do not advocate that the negro make politics or the holding of office an important thing in his life. I do urge, in the interest of fair play for everybody, that a negro who prepares himself in property, in intelligence, and in character to cast a ballot, and desires to do so, should have the opportunity. . . .

In most parts of the United States the colored people feel that they suffer more than others as the result of the lynching habit. . . .

Within the last twelve months there have been seventy-one cases of lynching, nearly all of colored people. Only seventeen were charged with the crime of rape. Perhaps they are wrong to do so, but colored people in the South do not feel that innocence offers them security against lynching. They do feel, however, that the lynching habit tends to give greater security to the criminal, white or black. When ten millions of people feel that they are not sure of being fairly tried in a court of justice, when charged with a crime, is it not natural that they should feel that they have not had a fair chance?

I am aware of the fact that in what I have said in regard to the hardships of the negro in this country I throw myself open to the criticism of doing what I have all my life condemned and everywhere sought to avoid; namely, laying over-emphasis on matters in which the negro race in America has been badly treated, and thereby over-looking those matters in which the negro has been better treated than anywhere else in the world.

Despite all any one has said or can say in regard to the injustice and unfair treatment of the people of my race at the hands of the white men in this country, I venture to say that there is no example in history of the people of one race who have had the assistance, the direction, and the sympathy of another race in all its efforts to rise to such an extent as the negro in the United States.

Notwithstanding all the defects in our system of dealing with him, the negro in this country owns more property, lives in better houses, is in a larger measure encouraged in business, eats better food, has more schoolhouses and churches, more teachers and ministers than any similar group of negroes anywhere else in the world.

9

Washington's Personal Philosophy

The following selections illustrate certain salient fea-
tures of Washington's personal philosophy and character: his pa-
tience, pragmatism, optimism, and humor.

I feel that we should confine ourselves largely to things that lie
within our power to remedy. We might state so many difficulties and
find a great deal of fault with a great many things, but we had better
give ourselves to matters that we can help. We can overcome prejudices in a quiet, patient way much better than by abuse. The power
of the mouth is not like the power of the object lesson.[1]

There is still doubt in many quarters as to the ability of the
Negro, unguided, and unsupported, to hew out his own path, and
put into visible, tangible, indisputable forms the products and signs
of civilisation. This doubt cannot be extinguished by mere abstract
arguments, no matter how ingeniously and convincingly advanced.
Quietly, patiently, doggedly, through summer and winter, sunshine
and shadow, by self-sacrifice, by foresight, by honesty and industry,
we must re-enforce arguments with results. One farm bought, one
house built, one home neatly kept, one man the largest tax-payer and
depositor in the local bank, one school or church maintained, one
factory running successfully, one truck garden profitably cultivated,
one patient cured by a Negro doctor, one sermon well preached, one
office well filled, one life cleanly lived—these will tell more in our
favor than all the abstract eloquence that can be summoned to plead
our cause. Our pathway must be up through the soil, up through

[1] *Montgomery Advertiser,* February 21, 1895. Clipping, Washington Papers.

swamps, up through forests, up through the streams and rocks; up through commerce, education, and religion! [2]

At a meeting of Methodist ministers in Minneapolis Washington said:

One of the principal results of the negro's ignorance of the English language is that he has confused the personal pronouns, "mine" and "thine." But as his knowledge of grammer grows, he is extricating himself from this confusion. [3]

Our race is emotional. The average black man can feel more in an hour than a white man can in a day. It is one of their hymns that says, "Give me Jesus and you take all the rest," and the white men are only too ready to take them at their word. [4]

An old Negro who had achieved a degree of success as a farmer appeared at a Tuskegee Conference to tell about the growing of cotton.

Someone in the audience from a distance got up and said: "Uncle, will you tell us your name?"
The old fellow arose and said:

Now, as you asks me for my name, I'll tell you. In de old days, before dis teacher came here, I lived in a little log cabin on rented land, and had to mortgage my crop every year for food. When I didn't have nothin' in dem days in my community, dey used to call me "Old Jim Hill." But now I'se out of debt; I'se de deeds for fifty acres of land; and I lives in a nice house wid four rooms that's painted inside and outside; I'se got some money in de bank; I'se a taxpayer in my com-

[2] *Working with the Hands: Being a Sequel to Up From Slavery* (New York, 1904), p. 29.
[3] Minneapolis *Journal*, February 3, 1896. Clipping, Washington Papers.
[4] Boston *Transcript*, July 11, 1896. Clipping, Washington Papers.

munity; I'se edicated by children. And now in my community, dey calls me "Mr. James Hill."

The old fellow not only learned to raise cotton during these ten years, but, so far as he was concerned, he had solved the race problem.[5]

We should see to it too that we not only emphasize in our work as teachers the opportunities that are before our race, but should also emphasize the fact that we ought to become a hopeful, encouraged race. There is no hope for any man or woman, whatever his color, who is pessimistic; who is continually whining and crying about his condition. There is hope for any people, however handicapped by difficulties, that makes up its mind that it will succeed, that it will make success the stepping stone to a life of success and usefulness.[6]

[5] "Chapters from My Experience," *World's Work*, XXI (January, 1911), 13853–54.
[6] Address to National Colored Teachers Association at St. Louis, July 30, 1911. Typed copy, Box 957, Washington Papers.

PART TWO

BOOKER T. WASHINGTON VIEWED
BY HIS CONTEMPORARIES

The White World Looks
at Washington

The following selections are representative of contemporary white opinion of Washington as a man and as race leader. They include newspaper comment on the Atlanta Address and the White House dinner and on Washington's racial program. An account of some of Washington's "darkey" stories which so amused white audiences and offended Negro intellectuals is included in an excerpt from a diary which Claude Bowers kept as a high school student. The selection "Mr. Dooley Speaks," in which the voluble Irishman created by Finley Peter Dunne talks of the White House dinner, is not only a commentary on that episode but a perceptive essay on white racial attitudes and race relations, North and South.

The remarks of the industrialist Andrew Carnegie, who was the principal benefactor of Tuskegee, are typical of the fulsome praise which white philanthropists heaped upon Washington. Scarcely less laudatory is the article by the publisher-editor Walter Hines Page, who published many of Washington's articles and books. Page, who was born in the South but who made his career in the North, asserts that through the system of industrial education Washington has found the answer to the race problem which has plagued the United States since its founding. William Dean Howells, one of the leading novelists of the era, calls Washington "an exemplary citizen." He praises his common sense and conservatism and lack of bitterness toward the white race. Howells asserts that, considering the circumstances of the times, in the face of the loss of political rights by Negroes, Washington's approach is the only way and that he displays "adroit" and "subtle" statesmanship. Washington, he says, does not have the intellectual stature of Frederick Douglass, and the career of

Douglass was of greater dynamic importance than that of Washington, but he doubts if Douglass would have been as able as Washington to deal with the realities of the post-Reconstruction South.

Most white contemporaries agreed that one of Washington's greatest achievements was his success in winning the confidence of the white South. Most southern newspapers supported his program and praised him as a safe and conservative leader. But there were some dissents among southern whites. An example is the article by Thomas Dixon, Jr., who is representative of the extreme champions of white supremacy. Dixon insists that industrial education and economic advancement of Negroes will not improve race relations but will lead to racial strife because they will bring Negroes into economic competition with whites. Moreover he asserts that Washington is concealing his ultimate objective, which is racial amalgamation, the bête noire of the white South.

The race problem in the United States was a matter of perennial interest to the British as well as to Americans. Washington and his program attracted a considerable amount of attention in Great Britian. As a visitor to that country he was received by many distinguished persons, including Queen Victoria, and given a number of opportunities to speak. British visitors to the United States were also interested in Tuskegee and its principal.

Below are selections by two distinguished British writers. The first, "The Tragedy of Color," by H. G. Wells, is part of on article in a series which he wrote while on a visit to the United States. The tragedy, he suggests, is caused by the ignorance and prejudice of white Americans. He gives a sympathetic picture of Washington and sees him, not as the optimist whom most whites saw, but a rather melancholy figure who endures with dignity and opposes with patience and restraint the indignities heaped upon his race because there is no alternative. The second selection is from Lord Bryce's American Commonwealth, which is regarded as a classic treatise on the United States and its institutions. Bryce visited the United States several times and served as British ambassador from 1907 to 1913. He consulted with Booker T. Washington on some of the material relating to the race situation in the revised edition of his work which appeared in 1910. The excerpt below is of interest because it illustrates the prevailing belief in inherent racial characteristics which was held even by dispassionate scholars like Bryce.

THE ATLANTA ADDRESS

There was a remarkable figure, tall, bony, straight as a Sioux chief, high forehead, straight nose, heavy jaws, and strong determined mouth, with big white teeth, piercing eyes and commanding manner. The sinews stood out on his bronze neck, and his muscular right arm swung high in the air with a lead pencil grasped in the clinched brown fist. His big feet were planted squarely, with the heels together and the toes turned out. His voice rang out clear and true, and he paused impressively as he made each point.

Within ten minutes the multitude was in an uproar of enthusiasm— handkerchiefs were waved, canes were flourished, hats were tossed in the air. The fairest women of Georgia stood up and cheered. . . .

I have heard the great orators of many countries, but not even Gladstone himself could have pleaded a cause with more consummate power than this angular Negro standing in a nimbus of sunshine surrounded by the men who once fought to keep his race in bondage. The roar might swell ever so high, but the expression of his earnest face never changed.[1]

But when all that is said, it remains true that the speech of the day was that of Mr. Washington. Even before he spoke he had the good will of the audience, which received him with hearty applause; but before he ended he had fairly taken the house off its feet. When he made a good point, and his address was full of good points, he was greeted with thunders of applause, when it was finished it was felt by everyone who listened to him, Southern as well as Yankee, that the appearance of such a man on such an occasion and in such a presence marked an epoch in the history of the South.[2]

In all respects it was the most remarkable address ever delivered by a colored man in America, for it was the first time that one of

[1] Article by James Creelman in New York *World*. Undated clipping, Washington Papers.

[2] New York *Tribune*, September 19, 1895. Clipping, Washington Papers.

that race ever took so prominent a part in any great national or international affair not of a political character. The speech stamps Booker T. Washington as a wise counselor and a safe leader.

It was a very dignified and eloquent oration, and if it could reach the hearts and minds of the colored people, it would undoubtedly accomplish great good.

And yet it was an address leveled at the whites. It will reach these and will go far toward narrowing, if not solving, the great problem known as the negro question. There never was any problem in this question until certain Northern politicians insisted that the property and intelligence of the South should be placed in charge of those who had neither property or intelligence. This was a little too much of a good thing, and out of it has grown what is called the negro problem. Professor Washington solves it in a few terse words, and what he says ought to illuminate the minds of those Northern philanthropists who imagine that the political advancement of the negro meant his social advancement.[3]

[One of the best speeches was made by a Negro.] It was striking for the breadth and practical character of the views expressed, showing that the negro, when really educated, in manners and morals as well as in book lore, is likely to be a reasonable, conservative person and not given to the assertion of unwelcome social pretensions.[4]

WASHINGTON'S HUMOR [5]

Oct. 20 [1897]. This afternoon as I was walking down Penn. St., I met Brooker [*sic*] T. Washington, reading a newspaper in front of The Denison. I talked with him for awhile. . . .

Tonight I heard him address a monster convention of the Christian church people. He is a magnificent orator—one of the Phillips type. His style is mostly conversational. Now and then as he becomes especially eloquent his voice rises and his form expands. His voice is

[3] Atlanta *Constitution,* September 20, 1895. Clipping, Washington Papers.

[4] Baltimore *Sun,* September 20, 1895. Clipping, Washington Papers.

[5] Holman Hamilton and Gayle Thornbrough, eds., *Indianapolis in the "Gay Nineties": High School Diaries of Claude G. Bowers* (Indianapolis, 1964), pp. 98–99. Copyright © 1964 by the Indiana Historical Society. Reprinted by permission of the Indiana Historical Society. Bowers later became a well-known historian through such books as *Jefferson and Hamilton* and *The Tragic Era.* He also served as United States Ambassador to Spain and Chile.

rough in the higher scale but that is lost sight of in what he says. He has a limitless store of original antedote [sic] gleaned from personal expierence [sic] with which he keeps his audience in a constant roar. I noticed one man on the platform—an old grey haired man—who went into fits over the stories. He would press his sides, stamp his feet, and scream with laughter. I took down a few of his stories which I here record.

"It's a mighty hard thing to make a good Christian out of a hungry man."

"The colored men down south are very fond of an old song entitled 'Give me Jesus and you take all the rest.' The white man has taken him at his word."

"A white man once asked a negro to loan him 3 cents to get across the river. The colored man replied 'Boss, I knows yous a white man, and Boss I knows yous got moah sense dan dis yeah niggah. But Boss I aint goin to lend you no three cents. Boss you say you haint got no money. Well Boss a man whats got no money is as well off on one side of the river as on de other . . .' "

"Weve got a few black sheep in our flock."

"A negro was once heard to say, 'Oh Lod, de sun am so hot, and de ground am so hard, and de sun am *so* hot, I believe dis heah darky am called to preach.' "

"A friend of mine who went to Liberia to study conditions once came upon a negro shut up with-in a hovel reading Cicero's orations. That was all right. The negro has as much right to read Cicero's orations in Africa as a white man does in America. But the trouble with the colored man was that he had on no pants. I want a tailor shop first so that the negro can sit down and read Cicero's orations like a gentleman with his pants on."

"I can't tell the exact day or place of my birth. But I have fairly conclusive evidence that I was born, some-time and some-where."

"There seems to be a sort of sympathy between the negro and a mule. Wherever you find a negro you are very apt to find a mule some-where about. I feel somewhat lonesome tonight. A colored man was once asked how many there were in the family. He replied, 'Five of us My-self, my brother and three mules.' "

"We were the only race that came here by special invitation. Your race came over here against the protest of the leading citizens. We were so important to your interest that you had to send for us at a great cost and inconvenience. Now that we have been brought here at so much cost, it would be very ungrateful for us not to oblige you by staying here."

"A slave was once called up before his master who thus addressed him—'Bill your soul belongs to God and your body belongs to me.' 'Yess—Hows dat mas'er?' 'Your soul belongs to God, and your body belongs to me.' 'Wars I come in mas'er?'

"One Sunday afterwards during a violent rain, Bill was seen running bare-headed through the rain—his hat tucked under his coat. His owner called him up and asked him why he did not put on his hat. 'Oh, mas'er, dis yeah niggahs soul belongs to God, my body belongs to mas'er, but de hat belongs to dis heah niggah.' "

THE WHITE HOUSE DINNER

Newspaper Comment

[The Memphis *Commercial Appeal* says that by inviting Washington to dinner President Theodore Roosevelt has accepted the Negro as his social equal.]

If he is sincere in his admission of social equality, he must also admit the propriety of negroes and whites intermarrying. But would President Roosevelt go this far? Would he give his daughter in marriage to Booker T. Washington's son? Not much. . . . The son of Booker Washington belongs to another and inferior race. . . .

The higher animal cannot safely consort with the lower. It is against nature. . . . Those who drag their own race to the level of the lower race are degenerate. It is true that there are some negroes who in character, in intellect, and in ability compare favorably with the whites; but this does not obliterate the fact of racial distinctions. There are educated horses, dogs and sea lions. We have even heard of educated fleas but this does not encourage us to admit them to personal contact or invite them into the parlor as it were.[6]

God set up the barrier between the races. No President of this or any other country can break it down. The news item which came from Washington and was printed in yesterday's Telegraph told a sad story for our country. We shall hear more of this.[7]

[6] Memphis *Commercial Appeal*, October 29, 1901.
[7] Macon *Telegraph*, quoted in Baltimore *Sun*, October 20, 1901.

[In a speech at Guthrie, Oklahoma, Senator Ben Tillman of South Carolina was quoted as saying:]

The action of President Roosevelt in entertaining that nigger will necessitate our killing a thousand niggers in the South before they learn their place again.[8]

If the President had invited a cultivated Indian, Hindoo, or Chinaman to dinner no Southerner would have objected. . . . But when a black gentleman is treated by the President as a white gentleman would be treated, then the thunders roll and fierce remarks are made, which, coming from intelligent men in the year 1901, are quite entertaining.[9]

Mr. Dooley Speaks [10]

"What ails th' prisdint havin' a coon to dinner at th' White House?" asked Mr. Hennessy.

"He's a larned man," said Mr. Dooley.

"He's a coon," said Mr. Hennessy.

"Well, annyhow," said Mr. Dooley, "it's goin' to be th' roonation iv Prisidint Tiddy's chances in th' South. Thousan's iv men who wudden't have voted f'r him undher anny circumstances has declared that under no circumstances wud they now vote f'r him. He's lost near ivry state in th' South. Th' gran' ol' commonwealth iv Texas has deserted th' banner iv th' raypublican party an' Mississippi will cast her unanimous counted vote again him. Onless he can get support fr'm Matsachoosetts or some other state where th' people don't care annything about th' naygur excipt to dislike him, he'll be beat sure. . . .

" 'Ye'll not be th' first Wash'nton that's et here,' he says. 'Th' other was no rilitive, or at laste,' says Booker T., 'he'd hardly own me,' he says. 'He might,' says th' prisidint, 'if ye'd been in th' neighborhood iv Mt. Vernon in his time,' he says. 'Annyhow,' he says, 'come up. I'm goin' to thry an experiment,' he says. 'I want to see will all th'

---

[8] Philadelphia *American,* October 24, 1901.

[9] *Chicago Daily Tribune,* October 19, 1901.

[10] [Finley Peter Dunne], *Mr. Dooley's Opinions* (New York, 1901), pp. 207–12. Dunne (1867–1936), a journalist and humorist, was one of the most perceptive and popular commentators on American politics and society. In his essays he used his creation, Mr. Dooley, the Irishman, as the instrument for his observations.

pitchers iv th' prisidints befure Lincoln fall out iv th' frames whin
ye come in,' he says. An' Booker wint. So wud I. So wud annywan.
I'd go if I had to black up.

"I didn't hear that th' guest done annything wrong at th' table.
Fr'm all I can larn, he hung his hat on th' rack an' used proper
discrimination between th' knife an' th' fork an' ast f'r nawthin'
that had to be sint out f'r. They was no mark on th' table cloth where
his hands rested an' an invintory iv th' spoons after his departure
showed that he had used gintlemanly resthraint. At th' con-clusion
iv th' fistivities he wint away, lavin' his ilusthrees friend standin'
on th' top iv San Joon hill an' thought no more about it. Th' ghost
iv th' other Wash'nton didn't appear to break a soop tureen over
his head. P'raps where George is he has to assocyate with manny
mimbers iv th' Booker branch on terms iv akequality. I don't suppose
they have partitions up in th' other wurruld like th' kind they have
in th' cars down south. They can't be anny Crow Hivin. I wondher
how they keep up race supreemacy. Maybe they get on without it.
Annyhow I wasn't worrid about Booker T. I have me own share
iv race prejudice, Hinnissy. . . . But this wasn't my dinner an' it
wasn't my house an' I hardly give it a thought.

"But it hit th' Sunny Southland. No part iv th' counthry can be
more gloomy whin it thries thin th' Sunny Southland an' this here
ivint sint a thrill iv horror through ivery newspaper fr'm th'
Pattymack to th' Sugar Belt. 'Fr'm time immemoryal,' says wan paper
I read, 'th' sacred rule at th' White House has been, whin it comes
to dinner, please pass th' dark meat.' It was a wise rule an' founded
on thrue principles. Th' supreemacy iv th' white depinds on socyal
supeeryority an' socyal supeeryority depinds on makin' th' coon ate
in th' back iv th' house. He raises our food f'r us, cooks it, sets th'
table an' brings in th' platter. We are liberal an' we make no attimpt
to supplant him with more intilligent an' wage labor. We encourage
his industhry because we know that f'r a low ordher iv intilligence,
labor is th' on'y panacee. It is no good f'r a thoughtful man. We
threat him right. He has plenty to do an' nawthin' to bother him an'
if he isn't satisfied he be hanged. . . . But whin it comes to havin'
him set down at th' table with us, we dhraw th' color line an' th' six
shooter. Th' black has manny fine qualities. He is joyous, light-
hearted, an' aisily lynched. But as a fellow bong vivant, not be anny
means. We have th' highest rayspict f'r Booker T. Wash'nton. He's
an idjacated coon. He is said to undherstand Latin an' Greek. We

do not know. But we know that to feed him at th' White House was an insult to ivery honest man an' fair woman in th' Sunny Southland an' a blow at white supreemacy. That must be avinged. . . .

"So there ye are. An' f'r th' life iv me, I can't tell which is right. But I think th' prisidint's place is a good dale like mine. I believe that manny an honest heart bates beneath a plaid vest, but I don't like a naygur. Howiver, Hinnissy, if Fate, as Hogan said, had condemned me to start in business on th' Levee, I'd sarve th' black man that put down th' money as quick as I wud th' white. I feel I wudden't, but I know I wud. But bein' that I'm up here in this Cawcasyan neighborhood, I spurn th' dark coin. . . . But black an' white don't mix, Hinnissy, an' if it wint th' rounds that Dooley was handin' out rayfrishmint to th' colored popylation, I might as well change me license. So be th' prisidint. They'se nawthin' wrong in him havin' me frind Booker T. up to dinner. That's a fine naygur man, an' if me an' th' presidint was in a private station, d'ye mind, we cud f'rget th' color iv th' good man . . . But bein' that I—an' th' prisidint—is public sarvants an' manny iv our customers has onrais'nable prejoodices, an' afther all 't is to thim I've got to look f'r me support. . . . 'Tis not me that speaks, Hinnissy, 't is th' job. Dooley th' plain citizen says, 'Come in, Rastus.' Dooley's job says: 'If ye come, th' r-rest will stay away.' An' I'd like to do something f'r th' naygur, too."

"What wud ye do?" asked Mr. Hennessy.

"Well," said Mr. Dooley, "I'd take away his right to vote an' his right to ate at th' same table an' his right to ride on th' cars an' even his sacred right to wurruk. I'd take thim all away an' give him th' on'y right he needs nowadays in th' South."

"What's that?"

"Th' right to live," said Mr. Dooley. "If he cud start with that he might make something iv himsilf."

NORTHERN OPINION

Andrew Carnegie [11]

The remaining vital negro political question is that of the suffrage. The National Constitution provides that no State shall dis-

---

[11] Andrew Carnegie, *The Negro in America. An Address Delivered Before the Philosophical Institute of Edinburgh* (Inverness, 1907), pp. 30, 31, 39–40.

criminate on account of color. Many of the Southern States now require ability to read and write, which applies to whites as well as blacks. The best people, both North and South, approve this educational test. One good effect is that it gives illiterates, both white and black, a strong inducement to educate themselves. . . .

Booker Washington's influence is powerfully exerted to keep the negroes from placing suffrage in the front. He contends that good moral character and industrial efficiency, resulting in ownership of property, are the pressing needs and the sure and speedy path to recognition and enfranchisement. A few able negroes are disposed to press for the free and unrestricted vote immediately. We cannot but hope that the wiser policy will prevail. . . .

Booker Washington is the combined Moses and Joshua of his people. Not only has he led them to the promised land, but still lives to teach them by example and precept how properly to enjoy it. He is one of these extraordinary men who rise at rare intervals and work miracles. Born a slave, he is today the acknowledged leader of his race—a modest, gentlemanly man, of pure, simple life and engaging qualities, supremely wise, an orator, organiser and administrator combined. Considering what he was and what he is, and what he has already accomplisht, the point he started from and the commanding position attained, he certainly is one of the most wonderful men living or who has ever lived. History is to tell of two Washingtons, the white and the black, one the father of his country, the other the leader of his race.

William Dean Howells [12]

Except for the race ignominy and social outlawry to which he was born, the story of Booker T. Washington does not differ so very widely from that of many another eminent American. His origin was not much more obscure, his circumstances not much more squalid, than Abraham Lincoln's, and his impulses and incentives to the making of himself were of much the same source and quality. . . . There is nothing more touching in his book than the passages which record her [his mother's] devotion and her constant endeavor to help him find the way so dark to her. There is nothing more beautiful and uplifting in literature than the tender reverence, the devout honor with which he repays her affection. His birth was a

---

[12] William Dean Howells, "An Exemplary Citizen," *North American Review*, CLXXIII (August, 1901), 281–88.

part of slavery, and she was, in his eyes, as blameless for its conditions as if it had all the sanctions. The patience, the fearless frankness, with which he accepts and owns the fact, are not less than noble; and it is not to their white fathers but to their black mothers, that such men as Frederick Douglass and Booker Washington justly ascribe what is best in their natures. . . .

Booker Washington early divined the secret of happiness as constant activity for the good of others. This was the first thing he learned from the example of the admirable man who became his ideal and his norm: he formed himself, morally at least, upon General Armstrong, and in a measure he studied his manner—his simple and sincere manner—oratorically.

This must be evident to any one who has heard both men speak. It was most apparent to me when I heard Mr. Washington speak at a meeting which had been addressed by several distinguished white speakers. When this marvelous yellow man came upon the platform, and stood for a moment, with his hands in his pockets, and with downcast eyes, and then began to *talk* at his hearers the clearest, soundest sense, he made me forget all those distinguished white speakers, and he made me remember General Armstrong, from whom he had learned that excellent manner. . . .

What strikes you first and last, in Mr. Washington is his constant common sense. He has lived heroic poetry, and he can, therefore, afford to talk simple prose. Simple prose it is, but of sterling worth, and such as it is a pleasure to listen to as long as he chooses to talk. It is infused with the sweet, brave humor which qualifies his writing, and which enables him . . . to place himself outside his race, when he wishes to see it as others see it, and to report its exterior effect from his interior knowledge. To do this may not be proof of the highest civilization, but it is a token of the happiest and usefullest temperament. . . .

The temper of his mind is conservative, and, oddly enough, that seems to be the temper of the Afro-American mind whenever it comes to its consciousness. The Anglo-American of the South may be, and often has been, an extremist, but the Afro-American, so far as he has made himself eminent, is not. Perhaps, it is his unfailing sense of humor that saves him from extremism. . . .

This calm is apparently characteristic of the best of the race, and in certain aspects it is of the highest and most consoling promise. It enables them to use reason and the nimbler weapons of irony, and saves them from bitterness. By virtue of it Washington, and Dunbar and Chesnutt[13] enjoy the negro's ludicrous side as the white observer enjoys it, and Douglass could see the fun of the zealots whose friend and fellow fighter he was. The fact has all sorts of interesting implications; but I will draw from it, for the present, the sole suggestion that the problem of the colored race may be more complex than we have thought it. What if upon some large scale they should be subtler than we have supposed? What if their amiability should veil a sense of *our* absurdities, and there should be in our polite inferiors the potentiality of something like contempt for us? The notion is awful; but we may be sure that they will be too kind, too wise, ever to do more than let us guess at the truth, if it is the truth.

Mr. Washington's experience of our race has been such as to teach him a greater measure of kindness for it than many of his race have cause to feel. . . . In his heart there is no bitterness. If his rights are taken away, he will work quietly on till they are given back. No doubt, it is the wisest way. If he keeps faithfully and quietly at work, he will presently be an owner of the earth and have money in the bank, and from such their rights cannot long be withheld. They can buy the strong arm that robs them; they can invoke the law to make the oppressor get off the land.

Mr. Washington's way seems, at present, the only way for his race, which has not even the unrestricted suffrage . . . as white labor has. . . . What is certain is that Mr. Washington has entire faith in his plan, and that, while he is not insensible or indifferent to the unlawful disabilities of his people, he sees no hope in their making a fight against them, and further alienating the stronger race about them. By precept and by practice he counsels, not a base submission to the Southern whites, but a manly fortitude in bearing the wrongs that cannot now be righted, and a patient faith in the final kindliness and ultimate justice of the Anglo-Americans, with whom and by whom the Afro-Americans must live. . . .

White men rise from squalor almost as great as that which has left no taint upon the mind and soul of the born thrall, Booker T. Washington. But it must be remembered to his honor, and to his greater glory as a fighter against fate, that they rise in the face of no odds as he has had to encounter. . . .

[13] Paul Laurence Dunbar was the best-known Negro poet of the period; Charles W. Chesnutt the best-known Negro novelist.

In spite of them, though never in defiance of them, Booker T. Washington has made himself a public man, second to no other American in importance. He seems to hold in his strong grasp the key to the situation; for if his notion of reconciling the Anglo-American to the Afro-American, by a civilization which shall not threaten the Anglo-American supremacy, is not the key, what is? He imagines for his race a civilization industrial and economical, hoping for the virtues which spring from endeavor and responsibility; and apparently his imagination goes no further. But a less deeply interested observer might justify himself in hoping for it, from the things already accomplished in art and literature, a civilization of high aesthetic qualities.

As for the man himself, whose winning yet manly personality and whose ideal of self-devotion must endear him to every reader of his book,[14] something remains to be said, which may set him a true perspective and a true relation to another great Afro-American. . . . Neither by temperament nor condition had Frederick Douglass the charm which we feel when Booker T. Washington writes or speaks. The time was against him. In that time of storm and stress, the negro leader was, perforce, a fighter. . . .

He was not gentle; his life had been ungentle; the logic of his convictions was written in the ineffaceable scars of the whip on his back. Of such a man you do not expect the smiling good humor with which Booker T. Washington puts the question of his early deprivations and struggles by. The life of Frederick Douglass was a far more wonderful life, and when it finds its rightful place in our national history, its greater dynamic importance will be felt.

Each of these two remarkable men wrought and is working fitly and wisely in time and place. It is not well to forget slavery, and the memory of Frederick Douglass will always serve to remind us of it and of the fight against it. But it is not well to forget that slavery is gone, and that the subjection of the negro race which has followed it does not imply its horrors. The situation with which Booker T. Washington deals so wisely is wholly different from the situation which Douglass confronted, and it is slowly but surely modifying itself. The mild might of his adroit, his subtle statesmanship . . . is the only agency to which it can yield. Without affirming his intellectual equality with Douglass, we may doubt whether Douglass would have been able to cope so successfully with the actual conditions, and we

[14] *Up From Slavery: An Autobiography* (New York, 1901).

may safely recognize in Booker T. Washington an Afro-American of unsurpassed usefulness, and an exemplary citizen.

Walter H. Page [15]

In a company of half a dozen men of wide experience in life, among them a merchant, a financier, the manager of a large corporation, and a man of letters, the conversation lately turned on living great men in the United States. Many interesting observations had been made about men of noteworthy success and of strong personalities, when one of the company said:

> "Great" is too vague a phrase. But I think that Mr. Booker T. Washington is the most *useful* citizen of the Republic. He has done several things of historical value. He has proved the constructive and executive ability of the Negro in a large way; he has worked out a successful plan for the building-up of his race; and he has done more to remove race-friction in the South than any other man of his generation. . . .

And the whole company agreed that he was, perhaps, the most useful man now living in the United States. . . .

The first time that I went to Tuskegee I was asked to make an address to the school on Sunday evening. I sat upon the platform of the large chapel and looked forth on a thousand colored faces, and the choir of a hundred or more behind me sang a familiar religious melody. . . .

I found myself in front of this extra-ordinary mass of faces, thinking not of them, but of that long and unhappy chapter in our country's history which followed the one great structural mistake of the Fathers of the Republic, thinking of the one continuous great problem that generations of statesmen had wrangled over. . . . I was thinking of this dark shadow that had oppressed every large-minded statesman from Jefferson to Lincoln. These thousand young men and women about me were innocent victims of it. I, too, was an innocent victim of it. The whole Republic was a victim of that fundamental error of

[15] Walter H. Page, "Booker T. Washington: The Characteristics of the Colored Leader Who Has Shown the Way to Solve the Hardest Problem of Our National Life," *Everybody's Magazine*, April, 1902, pp. 393–98. Page was editor and publisher of *World's Work*, one of the leading journals of opinion, and a partner in the firm Doubleday, Page, and Company, which published most of Washington's books. Page served as United States ambassador to Great Britain during the First World War.

importing Africa into America. I held firmly to the first article of my faith that the Republic must stand fast by the principle of manhood suffrage; but I recalled the wretched mess that Reconstruction had made of it. . . .

Every effort of philanthropy seemed to have miscarried, every effort at correcting abuses seemed of doubtful value, and the race difference was asserting itself more and more. . . . Then I saw clearly that the first way out of a century of blunders had been made by this man who stood beside me and was introducing me to this audience. Before me was the material he had used. All about me was the indisputable evidence that he had found the natural line of development. He had shown the way. Time and patience, and encouragement and work would do the rest. . . .

The plan itself is not a new one. . . . But Tuskegee is, nevertheless, a brand-new chapter in the history of the Negro, and in the history of the knottiest problem we have ever faced. It not only makes "a carpenter of man; it makes a man of a carpenter." In one sense, therefore, it is of greater value than any other institution for the training of men and women that we have, from Cambridge to Palo Alto. It is almost the only one of which it may be said that it points the way to a new epoch in a large area of our national life.

To work out the plan on paper, or at a distance—that is one thing. For a white man to work it out—that, too, is an easy thing. For a colored man to work it out in the South, where, in its constructive period, he was necessarily misunderstood by his own people as well as by the whites, and where he had to adjust it at every step to the strained race relations—that is so very different and more difficult a thing that the man who did it put the country under lasting obligations to him.

It was not and is not a mere educational task. Anybody could teach boys trades and give them an elementary education. Such tasks have been done since the beginning of civilization. But this task had to be done with the rawest of raw material, done with a menial race, done within the civilization of the dominant race, and so done as not to run across race lines and social lines that are the strongest forces in the community. It had to be done for the benefit of the whole community. It had to be done, moreover, without local help, in the face of the direst poverty, done by begging, and done in spite of the ignorance of one race and the deep-rooted prejudice of the other. . . .

No man living had a harder task, and a task that called for more wisdom to do it right. The true measure of Mr. Washington's success is, then, not his teaching the pupils of Tuskegee, nor even gaining the support of philanthropic persons at a distance, but this—that every Southern white man of character and of wisdom has been won to a cordial recognition of the value of the work. . . .

The race divergence under the system of miseducation was fast getting wider. Under the influence of the Hampton-Tuskegee idea the races are coming into a closer sympathy and into an honorable and helpful relation. As the Negro becomes economically independent, he becomes a responsible part of the Southern life; and the whites so recognize him. And this must be so from the nature of things. There is nothing artificial about it. It is social development in a perfectly natural way. . . .

To say that Mr. Washington has won the gratitude of all thoughtful Southern white men, is to say that he has worked with the highest practical wisdom at a large constructive task; for no plan for the up-building of the freedman could succeed that ran counter to Southern opinion. To win the support of Southern opinion and to shape it was a necessary part of the task; and in this he has so well succeeded that the South has a sincere and high regard for him. . . . It is well for our common country that the day is come when he and his work are regarded as highly in the South as in any other part of the Union. I think that no man of our generation has a more noteworthy achievement to his credit than this; and it is an achievement of moral earnestness and of strong character of a man, in a word, who has done a great national service.

Race Interpreter [16]

The remarkable success of Booker T. Washington's latest speaking-tour in the South emphasizes again his usefulness to the whole country. In this role as an interpreter of one race to another, pleading for harmony, mutual respect, and justice, he is performing a patriotic service which it would be hard to overestimate. One of the foremost white educators now at work in the South exclaimed on hearing of the details of Mr. Washington's recent trip through Tennessee: "Now

[16] "Booker Washington's Greatest Service," *The Nation,* LXXXIX (December 9, 1909), 560–61.

I believe there is going to be a revolution in the South in favor of the negro." Of the fifty thousand persons who, it is estimated, attended his meetings, nearly one-half were white; and in every case he was received with an enthusiasm which would have turned the head of any less balanced and sagacious leader.

Lest we be accused of exaggeration, we would remind our readers that Judge Floyd Estill, at Winchester, Tennessee, introduced Washington the negro, once a homeless and destitute wanderer, as "a fine type of the true Southern gentleman"; that Judge J. H. Price, another typical Southerner of high position, classed Booker Washington with the first President, with Thomas Jefferson, Madison, and Monroe, Lee, and other Virginia worthies, as among that state's most distinguished sons; and that Judge J. M. Steen of the Circuit Court introduced him with these words:

> We believe that as the patriarchs of old were inspired by God to lead their people out of the darkness into light, to guide them on the right road to right living and success, so he who is to speak to us tonight is inspired to lead his race to higher and better things. . . .

All of this is enough to make any man accustomed to the ravings of the ordinary Southern office-seeker, or fire-brand lecturer of the Tillman order, rub his eyes and ask whether a revolution is not actually at hand. Yet these compliments to Mr. Washington and his work were received with the heartiest approval by thousands of earnest white listeners.

Still, this turning to Mr. Washington by such men of prominence ought not to surprise us. It is just the better self of the South coming to the front. . . .

To come back to Mr. Washington, the greatest service he can render to-day is plainly not at Tuskegee, and not at the White House conferring as to appointments, but on the stump in the South. His bearing and popularity enable white men to speak out freely where it would sometimes be difficult to do so if the negro endorsed were less well known. . . . Mr. Washington is to-day a great interpreter and leader. This must be recognized, whether one agrees with him in all his views or not. It is just fifty years since the death of John Brown; who could have thought in 1859 that a colored man in 1909 would have so won the gratitude and esteem of the nation?

SOUTHERN OPINION

Washington a "Safe Negro"

From the day of his arrival at Tuskegee . . . Booker T. Washington has had the absolute confidence of the white people of that community. There is never a word of harsh criticism of him or his methods. He has been singularly imbued with a desire to cultivate good relations between the two races, and to be of lasting benefit to his own people. He is succeeding in both undertakings. There is nothing of the agitator about him. His ways are those of pleasantness and peace, and as far as his voice and example prevail there will always be the best of feeling between the white and black people of the country.

It is a blessing for the control of the colored schools to fall into the hands of such a man as Booker T. Washington. It can be said to his credit that colored teachers are found all over Alabama who were educated at his institution, and in every instance the white people commend them for instilling correct notions into their pupils and for impressing upon them the fact that they cannot prosper unless their white neighbors prosper and unless a proper understanding exists between them. It is infinitely better to have teachers who have such notions than to have those who would seek to create prejudice which would inevitably lead to trouble.[17]

*   *   *

He is an advocate of high morality, sublime ethics and bath tubs. And in proof of his good sense and sound reasoning he places the bath tub at the beginning.

Washington is extra-ordinary; he is so rare as to be a novelty. And, by the way, only Southerners can appreciate this. In the North he doubtless approximates an extravagant ideal; a Boston aunties' ideal of a well rounded African personality created especially to spite the South. To the South he is more than that. He is more solid than an ideality; he is substantial reality, and he has the glitter of contrast, like a diamond cast in a basket of charcoal. And such a personality does not spite the South nor pain it. Nor does it prove that the South's

---

[17] *Montgomery Advertiser,* quoted in Max Bennett Thrasher, *Tuskegee: Its Story and Its Work* (Boston, 1900), p. 193.

attitude toward the negro lacks the principle of encouragement. . . .
In fact, Washington is an exoneration of the South. He is too broad
to blame a section for the defects and shortcomings of his race.[18]

Thomas Dixon, Jr.[19]

For Mr. Booker T. Washington as a man and leader of his race
I have always had the warmest admiration. His life is a romance
which appeals to the heart of universal humanity. The story of a
little ragged, barefooted pickaninny who lifted his eyes from a cabin
in the hills of Virginia, saw a vision and followed it, until at last he
presides over the richest and most powerful institution of harmony
in the South, and sits down with crowned heads and Presidents, has
no parallel in the Tales of the Arabian Nights.

The spirit of the man, too, has always impressed me with its
breadth, generosity and wisdom. The aim of his work is noble and
inspiring. As I understand it from his own words, it is "to make
Negroes producers, lovers of labor, honest, independent, good." His
plan for doing this is to lead the Negro to the goal through the
development of solid character, intelligent industry and material
acquisition.

Only a fool or a knave can find fault with such an ideal. It rests
squarely on the eternal verities. And yet it will not solve the Negro
problem nor bring us within sight of its solution. Upon the other
hand, it will only intensify that problem's danger-features, complicate
and make more difficult its ultimate settlement.

It is this tragic fact to which I am trying to call the attention of
the nation.

I have for the Negro race only pity and sympathy. . . .

As a friend of the Negro race I claim that he should have the
opportunity for the highest, noblest and freest development of his
full, rounded manhood. He has never had this opportunity in America, either north or south, and he never can have it. . . .

My books are simply merciless records of conditions as they exist,
conditions that can have but one ending if they are not honestly
and fearlessly faced. The Civil War abolished chattel slavery. It did

---

[18] Memphis *Commercial Appeal,* July 20, 1900.
[19] Thomas Dixon, Jr., "Booker T. Washington and the Negro," *Saturday Evening Post,* August 19, 1905. Dixon, a former Baptist minister, is best known for his novels *The Leopard's Spots* and *The Clansman,* which portray the Negro as degraded and bestial.

not settle the Negro problem. It settled the Union question and
created the Negro problem. . . .

The truth which is gradually forcing itself upon thoughtful students
of our national life is that no scheme of education or religion can
solve the race problem, and that Mr. Booker T. Washington's plan,
however high and noble, can only intensify its difficulties.

This conviction is based on a few big fundamental facts, which no
pooh-poohing, ostrich-dodging, weak-minded philanthropy or political
cant can obscure.

The first one is that no amount of education of any kind, industrial,
classical or religious, can make a Negro a white man or bridge the
chasm of the centuries which separate him from the white man in
the evolution of human civilization. . . .

What contribution to human progress have the millions of Africans
who inhabit this planet made during the past four thousand years?
Absolutely nothing. . . .

I repeat, education is the development of that which is. Behold the
man whom the rags of slavery once concealed—nine millions strong!
This creature, with a racial record of four thousand years of in-
capacity, half-child, half-animal, the sport of impulse, whim and con-
ceit, pleased with a rattle, tickled with a straw, a being who, left to
his will, roams at night and sleeps in the day, whose native tongue
has framed no word of love, whose passions once aroused are as
the tiger's—equality is the law of our life!—when he is educated
and ceases to fill his useful sphere as servant and peasant, what are
you going to do with him?

The second big fact which confronts the thoughtful, patriotic
American is that the greatest calamity which could possibly befall
this Republic would be the corruption of our national character by
the assimilation of the Negro race. I have never seen a white man
with any brains who disputes this fact. I have never seen a Negro
of any capacity who did not deny it.

One thought I would burn into the soul of every young American
(and who thinks of a Negro when he says "American?")—this: Our
Republic is great not by reason of any amount of dirt we possess, or
the size of our census roll, but because of the genius of the race of
pioneer white freemen who settled this continent. . . .

What is the attitude of Mr. Booker T. Washington on this vital
issue? You will search his books and listen to his lectures in vain for
any direct answer. Why? Because, if he dared to say what he really

in his soul of soul believes, it would end his great career, both North and South. In no other way has he shown his talent as an organizer and leader of his people with such consummate skill as in the dexterity with which he has for twenty years dodged this issue, holding steadily the good-will of the Southern white man and the Northern philanthropist. He is the greatest diplomat his race has ever produced.

The trouble with Mr. Booker T. Washington's work is that he is really silently preparing us for the future heaven of Amalgamation— or he is doing something equally dangerous, namely he is attempting to build a nation inside a nation of two hostile races. In this event he is storing dynamite beneath the pathway of our children—the end at last can only be in bloodshed.

Mr. Washington is not training Negroes to take their place in any industrial system of the South in which the white man can direct or control him. He is not training his students to be servants and come at the beck and call of any man. He is training them all to be masters of men, to be independent, to own and operate their own industries, plant their own fields, buy and sell their own goods, and in every shape and form destroy the last vestige of dependence on the white man for anything. . . .

The Negro remains on this continent for one reason only. The Southern white man has needed his labor, and therefore has fought every suggestion of his removal. But when he refuses longer to work for the white man, then what? . . .

The point I raise is that education necessarily drives the races further and further apart, and Mr. Washington's brand of education makes the gulf between them if anything a little deeper. If there is one thing a Southern white man cannot endure it is an educated Negro. What's to be the end of it if the two races are to live forever side by side in the South?

Mr. Washington says: "Give the black man so much skill and brains that he can cut oats like the white man—then he can compete with him."

And then the real tragedy will begin. Does any sane man believe that when the Negro ceases to work under the direction of the Southern white man this . . . [white] race will allow the Negro to master his industrial system, take the bread from his mouth, crowd him to the wall and place a mortgage on his house? Competition is war—the most fierce and brutal of all its forms. Could fatuity reach a sublimer height than the idea that the white man will stand idly by and see this performance? What will he do when put to the test? He will do exactly what his white neighbor in the North does when the Negro threatens his bread—kill him! . . .

We have spent about $800,000,000 on Negro education since the war. One-half of this sum would have been sufficient to make Liberia a rich and powerful Negro state. Liberia is capable of supporting every Negro in America. Why not face this question squarely? We are temporizing and playing with it. All our educational schemes are compromises and temporary makeshifts. Mr. Booker T. Washington's work is one of noble aims. A branch of it should be immediately established at Monrovia, the capital of Liberia. A gift of ten millions would do this, and establish a colony of half a million Negroes, within two years. They could lay the foundation of a free black republic which within twenty-five years would serve our race problem on the only rational basis within human power. Colonization is not a failure. It has never been tried.

We owe this to the Negro. At present we are deceiving him and allowing him to deceive himself. He hopes and dreams of amalgamation, forgetting that self-preservation is the first law of Nature. Our present attitude of hypocrisy is inhuman toward a weaker race brought to our shores by the sins of our fathers. We owe him a square deal, and we will never give it to him on this continent.

TWO BRITISH OPINIONS

H. G. Wells [20]

I have attempted time after time to get some answer from the Americans I have met, the answer to what is to me the most obvious of questions. "Your grandchildren and the grandchildren of these people [Negroes] will have to live in this country side by side; do you propose, do you believe it possible, that they shall be living then in just the same relations that you and these people are living now; if you do not, then what relations do you propose shall exist between them?"

It is not too much to say that I have never once had the beginnings of an answer to this question. . . .

My globe-trotting impudence will seem, no doubt, to mount to its

[20] H. G. Wells, "The Tragedy of Color," *Harper's Weekly*, L (September 15, 1906), 1317–19.

zenith when I declare that hardly any Americans at all seem to be in the possession of the elementary facts with relation to this question. These broad facts are not taught, as of course they ought to be, in school, and what each man knows is picked up by the accidents of his own untrained observation, by conversation always tinctured by personal prejudice, by hastily read newspapers and magazine articles and the like. The quality of this discussion is variable, but on the whole pretty low. . . .

I certainly did not begin to realize one most important aspect of this question until I reached America. I thought of those eight millions as of men, black as ink. But when I met Mr. Booker T. Washington, for example, I met a man certainly as white in appearance as our Admiral Fisher, who is, as a matter of fact, quite white. A very large proportion of these colored people is more than half white. One hears a good deal about the high social origins of the Southern planters, very many derive undisputably from the first families of England. It is the same blood flows in these mixed colored peoples veins. [Sic] Just think of the sublime absurdity, therefore, of the ban. There are gentlemen of education and refinement, qualified doctors and lawyers, whose ancestors assisted in the Norman Conquest, and they dare not enter a car marked white and intrude upon the dignity of the rising loan-monger from Esthonia. . . .

But whatever aspect I recall of this great taboo that shows no signs of lifting, of this great problem of the future . . . there presently comes to my mind the browned face of Mr. Booker T. Washington, as he talked to me over our lunch in Boston.

He has a face rather Irish in type, and the soft slow negro voice. He met my regard with the brown sorrowful eyes of his race. He wanted very much that I should hear him make a speech, because then his words came better; he talked, he implied, with a certain difficulty. But I preferred to have his talking, and get not the orator—everyone tells me that he is an altogether great orator in this country where oratory is still esteemed—but the man.

He answered my questions meditatively. I wanted to know with an active pertinacity. What struck me most was the way in which his sense of the overpowering forces of race prejudice weighs upon him. It is a thing he accepts; in our time and condition it is not to be fought about. He makes one feel with an exaggerated intensity (though I could not even draw him to admit) its monstrous injustice. He makes no accusations. He is for taking it as a part of the present fate of his "people," and for doing all that can be done for them within the limit that it sets.

Therein he differs from Du Bois, the other great spokesman color has found in our time. Du Bois is more of the artist, less of the statesman; he conceals his passionate resentment all too thinly. He batters himself into rhetoric against these walls. He will not repudiate the clear right of the black man to every educational facility, to equal citizenship, and to equal respect. But Mr. Washington has statecraft. He looks before and after, and plans and keeps his counsel with the scope and range of a statesman. I use "statesman" in its highest sense; his is a mind that can grasp the situation and destinies of a people. . . .

I argued strongly against the view he seems to hold that black and white might live without mingling and without injustice, side by side. That I do not believe. Racial differences seem to me always to exasperate intercourse unless people have been trained to ignore them. . . . "You must repudiate separation," I said. "No peoples have ever yet endured the tension of intermingled distinctness."

"May we not become a peculiar people—like the Jews?" he suggested. "Isn't that possible?"

But there I could not agree with him. . . . The colored people . . . are not a community at all in the Jewish sense, but outcasts from a community. They are the victims of a prejudice that has to be destroyed. These things I urged, but it was, I think, empty speech to my hearer. I could talk lightly of destroying prejudice, but he knew better. It was the central fact of his life, a law of his being. He has shaped all his projects and policy upon that. Exclusion is inevitable. So he dreams of a colored race of decent and inaggressive [sic] men silently giving the lie to all the legend of their degradation. They will have their own doctors, their own lawyers, their own capitalists, their own banks—because the whites desire it so. But will the uneducated whites endure even so submissive a vindication as that? Will they suffer the horrid spectacle of free and self-satisfied negroes in decent clothing on any terms without resentment? . . .

"I wish you would tell me," I said abruptly, "just what you think of the attitude of white America towards you. Do you think it is generous?"

He regarded me for a moment. "No end of people help us," he said.

"Yes," I said; "but the ordinary man. Is he fair?"

"Some things are not fair," he said, leaving the general question alone. "It isn't fair to refuse a colored man a berth on a sleeping-car. If I happen to be a privileged person, they make an exception for me; but the ordinary educated colored man isn't admitted to a sleeping-car at all. If he has to go a long journey, he has to sit up all night. His white competitor sleeps. Then in some places, in the hotels and restaurants—it's all right here in Boston—but southwardly he can't get proper refreshments. All that's a handicap. . . .

"The remedy lies in education," he said; "ours—*and theirs*.

"The real thing," he told me, "isn't to be done by talking and agitation. It's a matter of lives. The only answer to it all is for colored men to be patient, to make themselves competent, to do good work, to live well, to give no occasion against us. We feel that. In a way it's an inspiration.

"There is a man here in Boston, a negro, who owns and runs some big stores, employs all sorts of people, deals justly. That man has done more good for our people than all the eloquence or argument in the world. . . . That is what we have to do—it is all we *can* do . . ."

Whatever America has to show in heroic living to-day, I doubt if she can show anything finer than the quality of the resolve, the steadfast efforts hundreds of black and colored men are making to-day to live blamelessly, honorably and patiently, getting for themselves what scraps of refinement, learning and beauty they may, keeping their hold on a civilization they are grudged and denied. They do it not for themselves only, but for all their race. Each educated colored man is an ambassador to civilization. [*sic*] They know they have a handicap, they are not exceptionally brilliant or clever people. Yet every such man stands, one likes to think, aware of his representative and vicarious character, fighting against foul imaginations, misrepresentations, injustice, insult, and the naive unspeakable meanness of base antagonists. Every one of them who keeps decent and honorable does a little to beat that opposition down.

But the patience the negro needs!

No, I can't help idealizing the dark submissive figure of the negro in the spectacle of America. He, too, seems to me to sit waiting—and waiting with a marvelous and simple-minded patience—for finer understandings and a nobler time.

James Bryce [21]

To understand how American ideas work in an African brain, and how American institutions are affecting African habits, one must consider what are the character and gifts of the negro himself.

He is by nature affectionate, docile, pliable, submissive, and in these respects most unlike the Red Indian, whose conspicuous traits are pride and a certain dogged inflexibility. He is seldom cruel or vindictive—which the Indian often is,—nor is he prone to violence, except when spurred by lust or drink. His intelligence is rather quick than solid; and though not wanting in a sort of shrewdness, he shows the childishness as well as the lack of self-control which belongs to the primitive peoples. . . . Such talent as he has runs to words; he learns languages easily and speaks fluently, but shows no capacity for abstract thinking, for scientific inquiry, or for any kind of invention. It is, however, not so conspicuously on the intellectual side that his weakness lies, as in the sphere of will and action. Having neither foresight nor "roundsight," he is heedless and unthrifty, easily elated and depressed, with little tenacity of purpose, and but a feeble will to better his condition. . . .

*   *   *

The negroes have ceased to take much interest in politics. . . .

With this result the whites are doubly, nay, trebly, satisfied. They are relieved from any fear of negro dominance. They declare that the negro is growing to be more industrious, orderly, and generally useful now when he has dropped all thoughts of politics, and they add that friendly relations between the races have become easier, because, as the negro is no longer challenging equality, they are less called upon to proclaim superiority. . . .

Among the leaders of the negroes themselves there is a difference of view and policy on the matter. Some, bitterly resenting the disfranchising provisions, try to keep up an opposition to them, although they see little or no prospect of getting them repealed. Others think it better to accept facts which they are powerless to alter, consoling themselves by the reflection that provisions which make the suffrage depend on education and property tend to stimulate the negro to raise himself to the tests prescribed for active citizenship. The bulk

[21] James Bryce, *The American Commonwealth*, 2 vols. (New York, 1910), II, 517–18, 546–47, 552–55.

of the coloured people who live on the plantations take no interest in the matter. Among the more educated, the authority of Dr. Booker Washington has gone some way to commend the policy of preferring industrial progress to political agitation; not to add that it is hard to see what agitation could accomplish. . . .

Broadly speaking, there are two tendencies at work among the Southern whites, which correspond to the two classes of which Southern society consists.

The lower and more ignorant whites . . . dislike the negroes, desiring to thrust them down and to keep them down, and, so far as they can, to deny them civil rights as well as social opportunities. . . .

The cultivated and progressive white people of the South, including most, though not quite all, of the leading business men and professional men, and many of the large landowners, cherish more kindly feelings. . . .

But it must be remembered that upon some things all Southern whites are agreed. They all dread intermarriage. They all deem absolute social separation as necessary to prevent mixture of blood. . . . They all desire to prevent the negro vote from being a factor in politics, though some would concede the suffrage to the few who have education and property. And they would all alike resent the slightest interference by the National Government in any matter which concerns their State legislation, political or social, upon questions affecting the coloured race.

When one comes to speak of the views and attitude of the negroes themselves, it is necessary to premise that only a small percentage have any views at all. Even among those who can read and write, the number with sufficient knowledge or intelligence to comprehend the whole situation is small. . . .

Among the small class of educated and reflective negroes one may distinguish two tendencies. Reference has already been made to the opposite views of those who counsel acquiescence in, and of those who would agitate against, the restriction of the suffrage to a small section of their race. The divergence of views, however, goes further. There are those led by Dr. Booker Washington, who see no use in resisting patent facts, and therefore hold that all the negro can at present do, and the most effective thing that, with a view to the future, he could in any case do, is to raise himself in intelligence, knowledge, industry, thrift, whatever else makes for self-help and self-respect. When he has gained these things, when he is felt to be a valuable part of the community, his colour will not exclude him from the opportunities of advancement which business presents, nor from the suffrage, nor from a share in public office. Complaints of injustice, well grounded as many of them may be, will profit little, and may even rouse further antagonism, but industrial capacity and the possession of property are sure to tell.

Others there are, such as Professor Du Bois, who find it hard to practise this patience; and some are beginning to organize themselves in a more aggressive spirit for common help and protection.

The Negro World Looks
at Washington

Negro intellectuals were in most cases critical, or at least skeptical, of Washington and his influence, and since they were more articulate and better able to make their views known than were the Negro masses a disproportionate amount of the contemporary writing by Negroes which survives is from the anti-Washington group. On the other hand, while most Negro newspapers, with a few notable exceptions, were favorable to the Tuskegeean and his program, they are not necessarily a reliable index of popular opinion because so many of them were subsidized in one way or another by Washington.

The intellectuals criticized Washington on a number of scores. One of their principal charges was that his system of industrial education was intended to keep Negroes in a menial position and perpetuate the caste system. They felt that his seeming disparagement of academic training limited opportunities for higher education for talented Negroes and the development of Negro leaders. They resented his "darkey" stories because they reinforced the whites' belief in the stereotype of a childlike, backward, shiftless race. They were bitterly critical of his deprecatory remarks about political activity, his seeming defense of disfranchisement, and his acquiescence in segregation. Most of all, some of them resented the fact that in the eyes of the white world Washington held a near monopoly of Negro leadership, that he was regarded as the spokesman for the entire race and was therefore able to wield unchallenged power over the distribution of white philanthropy to Negro institutions and political appointments of Negroes. Because of his untiring efforts to conciliate the whites and because he usually said what the white world wanted to hear, Washington was accused of betraying the interests of his race for his own advancement. On the other hand, pro-Washington Negroes praised him because he was able to win the confidence of whites in both North and South.

In the following selections a number of well-known Negro contemporaries of Washington express their views of his program and his claims to race leadership. The first writer is T. Thomas For-

tune, editor of the New York Age, who like Washington had been born a slave. Although largely self-educated, he was regarded as the most able Negro journalist of the period. Fortune was known as a militant and uncompromising champion of Negro rights, but he was nevertheless for many years one of Washington's closest advisers and most loyal defenders. The second writer is Charles W. Chestnutt, a successful Negro novelist, who lived in Cleveland and moved freely in white circles. In the selections below, he lauded Washington for his success in establishing Tuskegee although he questioned his extreme emphasis on industrial education. He agreed with Washington that it was desirable for the Negro to win the good will of the white South, but unlike Washington, Chestnutt insisted that political rights are of fundamental importance and he was sharply critical of some of the Tuskegeean's remarks on suffrage and his seeming endorsement of the voting requirements in the new state constitutions of the South.

Probably Washington's most extreme and unremitting critic was William Monroe Trotter, who once spent a month in jail as a result of his efforts to challenge Washington and disrupt a meeting in Boston where he was speaking. Month after month he castigated the Tuskegeean in the columns of the Boston Guardian. *The selections below are examples which show the principal charges on which he indicted Washington for allegedly betraying his race. Another severe critic was Ida Wells Barnett, who, incidentally, was an ardent suffragette and feminist as well as a champion of Negro equality. She was especially well known for her efforts to arouse public opinion against lynching. In the article below she expressed the resentment which many educated Negroes felt at Washington's stories about Negroes. More important, she expressed their conviction that because of Washington's influence opportunities for higher education for Negroes were jeopardized.*

W. E. B. DuBois was Washington's most able and influential critic, partly because he was virtually the only Negro besides Washington who had access to publication in white periodicals and who was able to reach a white audience. Below are two selections in which he discusses Washington and his role. The first is part of the essay published in 1903 in which for the first time he publicly criticized Washington. In the second, published long after Washigtonn's death, he reiterated some of the same criticisms and dealt with the "Tuskegee Machine" and Washington's efforts to stifle criticism.

T. THOMAS FORTUNE

In the following selections the Negro editor T. Thomas For-tune defends Washington.

Is He the Negro Moses?

Booker Washington of Alabama

Who Has Leaped Into Fame

Born a Slave He Has Become Spokesman of 10,000,000 People—

Indeed of the Whole South

When Booker T. Washington stood up before the assembled wealth and culture and beauty of the South at Atlanta, Ga., Sept. 18, 1895, to make a speech at the opening day exercises of the Atlanta Exposition, it was an object lesson for all the world. The whole distance of thirty years of freedom, from the Appomattox of slavery's death to the Atlanta of freedom's making out of the devastation and desolation of Sherman's march to the sea, was measured. It marked the passing away of the slave-master spirit summed up in Chief Justice Taney's decision in 1856, that "it is held to be good law and precedent that the black man has no rights which a white man is bound to respect." . . . It marked the reversal of the long prevalent belief in the South that the Afro-American was incapable of the mental grasp and development of the Anglo-Saxon. It was also a proclamation that the black man is a living, positive factor in the intellectual and industrial conditions of the Southern states and of the republic, and entitled to the same fair and honorable condition enjoyed by the white man.[22]

* * *

[The Washington *Bee* insists that Booker T. Washington is an "apologist":]—in that he apologizes to the white people for the short comings of the Afro-American and misrepresents the race. If he told what the race is, and what the race can do, and did not cite isolated cases detrimental to Afro-Americans to tickle the fancy of the Caucasian, we would say that he is a benefactor. . . .

[22] New York *Sun,* October 13, 1895.

He is advocating a doctrine that depreciates the Afro-American in the estimation of the American white people and endeavoring to show that he is incapable of higher education.

In the columns of the New York Age, *T. Thomas Fortune replied.*

Mr. Washington has never exaggerated the condition of ignorance and poverty of the people among whom he labors, because he cannot do it. Their condition cannot be exaggerated, because the descriptive power of Dante or Milton or Butler or Dickens would fail to do it. As the editor of *The Bee* has never lived in the South or visited there as Mr. Washington has done and as the editor of *The Age* has done and is doing now, he can have no personal knowledge of the conditions with which Mr. Washington has to deal and which he seeks with Spartan courage . . . to better.[23]

In an interview with Fortune, a Boston Globe *reporter pointed out that the newspapers of the country frequently contrasted the positions of Fortune and Washington on the race question. He asked Fortune: "Is there any antagonism between your views and in your personal relations?"*
Fortune replied:

There is no difference whatever on our basic views in the race question. He [Washington] is naturally conservative in his views in all questions, while I am naturally radical.

He speaks always from the point of view of a leader who lives and labors in the South, and who believes that in order to gain one point in manhood development something can well be yielded upon another, and that we are to depend mostly upon education, property and

[23] Quoted in the Washington *Bee,* January 1, 1897. Calvin Chase, the editor of the *Bee,* which was one of the leading Negro newspapers, was for a number of years hostile to Washington, but later became more favorable to him and his program. There is evidence that in later years the *Bee* received some financial support from Washington.

character to pave our way to success; while I speak from the standpoint of a man who lives and labors in the North, and who does not believe in sacrificing anything that justly belongs to the race of manhood or constitutional rights.

Perhaps in the history of mankind more victories have been won through the policy of conservatism and moderation pursued by Mr. Washington than through the radical and unbending policy I have always pursued; but it is the temperament of the two of us, and we can neither of us change our nature.

I naturally regard Mr. Washington as the strongest and safest leader we have. The estimation in which he is held by the whites of the North is no greater than that in which he is held by the whites of the South. A man in that position cannot but be a great power for good.[24]

* * *

There are those of his own race who deny that Booker Washington is a leader of his race; that he stands in the place where Frederick Douglass stood; but there are none who can deny that he is the connecting link between the white people and the black people of the Southern States today, a link that makes for peace and amity and good will, and that in all the country there is no Afro-American wiser or stronger or more eloquent or more self-contained than he. The great Douglass when he spoke had no greater or more appreciative audience than Booker Washington. Neither black men nor white men placed him in this pre-eminent but perilous position; he placed himself there by supreme devotion to his race, by persuasive eloquence, by a wisdom tempered with studied conservatism, bristling "with malice toward none, with charity for all," as the immortal Lincoln expressed it in his second inaugural address and while standing in the shadow of the grave.

"I propose that no man shall drag me down by making me hate him," says Mr. Washington. "No race can hate another without itself being narrowed and hated." Again: "I thank God I have grown to the point where I can sympathize with a white man as much as I can with a black man; where I can sympathize with a Southern white man as much as with a Northern white man."

A leadership based on such philosophy as this does not necessarily need any particular race to sustain it; it is capable of standing upon its own merits, because it appeals to the human family and not to any

---

[24] Boston *Globe*, January 14, 1899.

fraction of it. And this is the essence of leadership, that it rises above race and comprehends the whole human family in its philosophy. Measured by this standard, what man of his race, past or present, can be compared to Booker Washington? What white man, in the North or the South, measures up to it?

When Booker Washington stood in his place at the Atlanta Exposition, pleading that white men and black men cast down their buckets where they stood, not looking afar off for the water of life when they were surrounded by a vast river of it, he revealed himself to the nation as a leader out of the forge of slavery who had laid the foundation deep in the hearts of the people of the black belt by the faith that wrought great works, that created something out of nothing. He stood forth as a finished orator who had burnt the midnight oil not studying alone the learning of the closet, but living, breathing men. No man revealed him; he revealed himself. . . .

It is fortunate for the country and for the Afro-American race at this time, when the relations of the races are lashed to fury by the wild storms of passion and momentary abdication of reason, that a man so capable and self-contained as Booker Washington should be recognized by the people of the country as the highest possible example of what his race is capable of. And a race which can give to freedom out of the death house of slavery two such men as Frederick Douglass and Booker T. Washington need not despair of its future, nor need those who wish it well despair of it.[25]

CHARLES W. CHESNUTT

A Plea for the American Negro [26]

Mr. Booker T. Washington has secured so strong a hold upon the public attention and confidence that anything he has to say in his chosen field is sure to command the attention of all who are interested in the future of the American negro. This volume [*The Future of the American Negro*], which is Mr. Washington's first extended utterance in book form, cannot fail to enhance his reputation for ability, wisdom,

[25] Boston *Transcript,* July 5, 1899.
[26] Charles W. Chesnutt, "A Plea for the American Negro," *The Critic*, XXXVI (1899), pp. 160–62. This article was a review of Washington's book *The Future of the American Negro.* A good biography of Chesnutt is Helen M. Chesnutt, *Charles Waddell Chesnutt, Pioneer of the Color Line* (Chapel Hill, 1952).

and patriotism. It is devoted to a somewhat wide consideration of the race problem, avoiding some of its delicate features, perhaps, but emphasizing certain of its more obvious phases. The author has practically nothing to say about caste prejudice, the admixture of the races, or the remote future of the negro, but simply takes up the palpable problem of ignorance and poverty as he finds it in the South, and looking neither to the right nor the left, and only far enough behind to fix the responsibility for present conditions, seeks to bring about such immediate improvement in the condition of the negro, and such a harmonious adjustment of race relations, as will lay the foundation for a hopeful and progressive future for the colored people. The practical philosophy of the book is eminently characteristic; it fairly bristles with the author's individuality.

As might be expected, much of the volume is devoted to discussing the importance of industrial education for the negro, of which the author is the most conspicuous advocate. . . . The argument for industrial education is not based upon any theory of the inferiority of the negro, which is beside the question, but upon the manifest conditions under which he must seek his livelihood. . . . It is to the building up of a substantial middle-class, so to speak, that industrial education and the lessons of industry and thrift inculcated by Mr. Washington are directed. He insists, somewhat rigidly, on the rational order of development, and is pained by such spectacles as a rosewood piano in a log schoolhouse, and a negro lad studying a French grammar in a one-room cabin. It is hardly likely that Mr. Washington has suffered very often from such incongruities, and some allowance should be made for the personal equation of even a negro lad in the Black Belt. Abraham Lincoln came out of a one-room cabin, and it would hardly have been a serious misfortune for him to have had a knowledge of French, or even of the piano. The world is wide, and the ambitious negro lad might move to some part of it where his knowledge of French or music would prove a very useful acquirement.

Mr Washington is a pioneer in another field. He has set out to gain for his race in the South, in the effort to improve their condition, the active sympathy and assistance of the white people in that section. This is perhaps a necessary corollary to his system of education, for it is in the South that he advises the negroes to stay, and it is among their white neighbors that they must live and practise the arts they acquire. If Mr. Washington succeeds in this effort, he will have solved the whole problem. But he has undertaken no small task. . . . The stu-

dent of history and current events can scarcely escape the impression
that it is the firm and unwavering determination of the Southern
whites to keep the negro in a permanent state of vassalage and subordination. . . .

It is to be hoped that Mr. Washington may convince the South that
the policy of Federal non-interference, which seems to be the attitude
of the present and several past administrations, places a sacred trust
upon the South to be just to the negro. . . .

There will undoubtedly be a race problem in the United States,
with all its attendant evils, until we cease to regard our colored population as negroes and consider them simply as citizens. . . . In the
meantime, if the work led by Mr. Washington shall succeed in promoting better conditions, either by smoothing over asperities; by appealing to the dormant love of justice which has been the crowning
glory of the English race—a trait which selfishness and greed have
never entirely obscured; or by convincing the whites that injustice is
vastly more dangerous to them than any possible loss of race prestige,
Mr. Washington will deserve, and will doubtless receive, the thanks of
the people of this whole nation.

The Disfranchisement of the Negro [27]

The argument of peace-loving Northern white men and Negro
opportunists that the political power of the Negro having long ago been
suppressed by unlawful means, his right to vote is a mere paper right,
of no real value, and therefore to be lightly yielded for the sake of a
hypothetical harmony, is fatally shortsighted. . . .

At present even good Northern men, who wish to educate the Negroes, feel impelled to buy this privilege from the none too eager
white South, by conceding away the civil and political rights of those
whom they would benefit. They have, indeed, gone farther than the
Southerners themselves in approving the disfranchisement of the
colored race. Most Southern men, now that they have carried their
point and disfranchised the Negro, are willing to admit, in the language of a recent number of the *Charleston Evening Post,* that "the
attitude of the Southern white man toward the Negro is incompatible
with the fundamental ideas of the republic." It remained for . . . the

[27] Charles W. Chesnutt, "The Disfranchisement of the Negro," in *The Negro
Problem: A Series of Articles by Representative American Negroes of Today* (New
York, 1903), pp. 96, 109–11.

most distinguished Negro leader to declare that "every revised Constitution throughout the Southern States has put a premium upon intelligence, ownership of property, thrift and character." So does every penitentiary sentence put a premium upon good conduct; but it is poor consolation to the one unjustly condemned, to be told that he may shorten his sentence somewhat by good behavior. Dr. Booker T. Washington, whose language is quoted above, has, by his eminent services in the cause of education, won deserved renown. If he has seemed, at times, to those jealous of the best things for their race, to decry the higher education, it can easily be borne in mind that his career is bound up in the success of an industrial school; hence any undue stress which he may put upon that branch of education may safely be ascribed to the natural zeal of the promoter, without detracting in any degree from the essential value of his teachings in favor of manual training, thrift and character-building. But Mr. Washington's prominence as an educational leader, among a race whose prominent leaders are so few, has at times forced him, perhaps reluctantly, to express himself in regard to the political condition of his people, and here his utterances have not always been so wise nor so happy. He has declared himself in favor of a restricted suffrage, which at present means, for his own people, nothing less than complete loss of representation—indeed it is only in that connection that the question has been seriously mooted; and he has advised them to go slow in seeking to enforce their civil and political rights, which, in effect, means silent submission to injustice. Southern white men may applaud this advice as wise, because it fits in with their purposes; but Senator McEnery of Louisiana, in a recent article in the *Independent*, voices the Southern white opinion of such acquiescence when he says: "What other race would have submitted so many years to slavery without complaint? *What other race would have submitted so quietly to disfranchisement?* These facts stamp his (the Negro's) inferiority to the white race." The time to philosophize about the good there is in evil, is not while its correction is still possible, but, if at all, after all hope of correction is past. Until then it calls for nothing but rigorous condemnation. To try to read any good thing into these fraudulent Southern constitutions, or to accept them as an accomplished fact, is to condone a crime against one's race. Those who commit crime should bear the odium. It is not a pleasing spectacle to see the robbed applaud the robber. Silence was better.

WILLIAM MONROE TROTTER [28]

In the following passages from the Boston Guardian *Trotter excoriates Washington.*

If Mr. Booker Washington is in any sense the leader of the Colored American people he certainly has been chosen for that position by the white American race. Everyone will admit that the Colored people never have chosen or indeed acclaimed him leader. Even Washington's friends will admit that his start for leadership came after his Atlanta speech in 1895, and that speech certainly was not popular with the Colored race.

He has been kept in a position as leader by the active work of the white race, with whom he has been extraordinarily popular, North and South. Their churches, their clubs, their pulpits, their press have boomed him and insisted he was the leader of his race. Mr. Washington has evidently realized this for he has always gone out of his way to say things that would suit prejudiced or race-proud white people, and he has been perfectly reckless as to the favor of his own race. In fact, at first he utterly ignored his own race, and only when told that he was valuable to the whites in so far as he induced his own people to follow his advice, did he begin to speak before them, and seek their favor, and endorsement. His sayings have been so hostile to his own race's wishes that his endeavor to get their endorsement has appeared to many to be unreasonable, in fact, a piece of effrontery. And it is no wonder that a man who talks as he does finds himself compelled to use money and school and political patronage, threats and persecution, abetted by his white supporters in order to get Negro endorsement, or stop Negro opposition.

This rule of races as to leaders was emphasized when Mr. Washington failed to drop his claims to leadership after accepting a life pension from a prominent member of the white race.[29] The insistence of the whites on Negroes accepting him as leader after this was remark-

[28] *Guardian* (Boston), January 9, July 6, July 30, 1904. For an account of Trotter's career, see Charles W. Puttkamer and Ruth Worthy, "William Monroe Trotter, 1872–1934," *Journal of Negro History,* XLIII (October, 1958), 298–316.
[29] This is a reference to the gift which Andrew Carnegie made to Washington to insure him and his wife an income during their lifetimes.

able, a palpable sign that they intended to master the Colored Race by means of Mr. Washington. And meantime Mr. Washington was upholding the South's devices of disfranchisement, and excusing their civil discriminations.

* * *

Eight years . . . [ago] Mr. Booker T. Washington, then a more or less obscure money beggar for a little known industrial school in Alabama, made a speech as a representative of the Negroes of the South, before a large white audience at Atlanta, Ga. In this speech he said, among other things, in criticism of his race, "The Negro made a mistake. He began at the Senate instead of the plow," and again, "It is a good thing to possess rights, but a better thing to deserve them." These statements, made to the very people who, once having held the Negro in slavery, had after they had been wrested from them, sought to re-enslave them by "black laws" which meant forced labor, and then when the national government vested them with citizenship and the ballot to save their lives, refused to join with them in the governing of the state, and finally, after getting the federal troops removed by specious promises of fair treatment, stripped them of every civil and political right, subjecting them to brutal treatment and exposing them to lynch law, were hailed with tremendous approbation by the white South. They gave color to the claim of the South that reconstruction was a blunder and that the Negro deserved the treatment they meted out to him. They were shrewd enough to see the value of such corroboration from a representative Negro and one engaged in educating his race.

But strange and sad to say for the Negro, these statements, thus cleverly phrased, struck a responsive cord in the northern white mind. . . .

Mr. Washington . . . who had leaped with one bound into tremendous popularity, took the cue. He continued the propaganda. His doctrine of limited education created a feeling of racial inferiority which was strengthened by the fun he made of the race in the degrading "darkey" stories. . . . He gave the impression that the southern whites were fair to the Negroes. He never made mention of the wrongs of his race. He ever and anon lauded the benefits of slavery. . . .

Not content with thus undermining northern sentiment in support of resistance to loss of civil rights by Negroes, he made a systematic campaign against agitation by Negroes. He repeatedly declared that "one large taxpayer in a community, one successful grocery," etc. was worth more to the race than all the eloquence that could be summed up to plead our cause. . . .

Mr. Washington has shown himself to be opposed to criticism, to do all in his power to destroy any agency of Negro criticism. . . . Any Negro in the land can be criticized and censured as to his public utterances in the colored press with impunity except Mr. Washington.

*   *   *

He has ridiculed the right and privilege of suffrage, until every Southern state has passed laws disfranchising Colored men; he has belittled the abominable effect of the separation of passengers on common carriers, and Jim Crow cars roll into and about the capitol on all sides without let or hindrance; he has found so much to praise in debasing human slavery that peonage and other involuntary servitude are fast becoming the rule rather than the exception in the practice of Southern states; he has sneered at higher education until state after state has indicated its purpose to limit the education of Negro children to the most rudimentary branches of knowledge. . . . Thus, as far as lay in his power [he has] aided and abetted the closing of the door of hope and of high opportunity to the Negro race South. . . .

And yet the camp followers of Washington, the most hurting obstacle to Negro progress today, say to us that we should cease our opposition to him. We shall cease when the sweet salt sea ceases to dash the shores of our bay yonder. By a great price obtained we this freedom, and no man shall barter it away.

IDA WELLS BARNETT [30]

Industrial education for the Negro is Booker T. Washington's hobby. He believes that for the masses of the Negro race an elementary education of the brain and a continuation of the education of the hand is not only the best kind, but he knows it is the most popular with the white South. He knows also that the Negro is the butt of ridicule with the average white American, and that the aforesaid American enjoys nothing so much as a joke which portrays the Negro as illiterate and improvident; a petty thief or a happy-go-lucky inferior. The average funny paragrapher knows no other class. . . . Booker

[30] Ida Wells Barnett, "Booker T. Washington and His Critics," *The World Today,* April, 1904, pp. 518–21.

T. Washington . . . knows, as do all students of sociology, that the representatives which stand as the type for any race, are chosen not from the worst but from the best specimens of that race; the achievements of the few rather than the poverty, vice and ignorance of the many, are the standards of any given race's ability. . . .

That one of the most noted of their own race should join with the enemies to their highest progress in condemning the education they had received, has been to . . . [college educated Negroes] a bitter pill. And so for a long while they keenly, though silently, resented the gibes against the college-bred youth which punctuate Mr. Washington's speeches. He proceeds to draw a moral therefrom for his entire race. The result is that the world which listens to him and which largely supports his educational institution, has almost unanimously decided that college education is a mistake for the Negro. They hail with acclaim the man who has made popular the unspoken thought of that part of the North which believes in the inherent inferiority of the Negro, and the always outspoken southern view to the same effect. . . .

No human agency can tell how many black diamonds lie buried in the black belt of the South, and the opportunities for discovering them become rarer every day as the schools for thorough training become more cramped and no more are being established. The presidents of Atlanta University and other such schools remain in the North the year round, using their personal influence to secure funds to keep these institutions running. Many are like the late Collis P. Huntington, who had given large amounts to Livingston College, Salisbury, North Carolina. Several years before his death he told the president of that institution that as he believed Booker Washington was educating Negroes in the only sensible way, henceforth his money for that purpose would go to Tuskegee. All the schools in the South have suffered as a consequence of this general attitude, and many of the oldest and best which have regarded themselves as fixtures now find it a struggle to maintain existence. As another result of this attitude of the philanthropic public, and this general acceptance of special educational standards for the Negro, Tuskegee is the only endowed institution for the Negro in the South. . . .

Does this mean that the Negro objects to industrial education? By no means. It simply means that he knows by sad experience that industrial education will not stand him in place of political, civil and intellectual liberty, and he objects to being deprived of fundamental rights of American citizenship to the end that one school for industrial training shall flourish. To him it seems like selling a race's birthright for a mess of pottage.

They [sic] believe it is possible for Mr. Washington to make Tuskegee all it should become without sacrificing or advocating the sacrifice of race manhood to do it. . . .

The demand from this class of Negroes is growing that if Mr. Washington can not use his great abilities and influence to speak in defense of and demand for the rights withheld when discussing the Negro question, for fear of injury to his school by those who are intolerant of Negro manhood, then he should be just as unwilling to injure his race for the benefit of his school. They demand that he refrain from assuming to solve a problem which is too big to be settled within the narrow confines of a single system of education.

W. E. BURGHARDT DU BOIS

Of Mr. Booker T. Washington and Others [31]

Easily the most striking thing in the history of the American Negro since 1876 is the ascendancy of Mr. Booker T. Washington. It began at the time when war memories and ideals were rapidly passing; a day of astonishing commercial development was dawning; a sense of doubt and hesitation overtook the freedmen's sons,—then it was that his leading began. Mr. Washington came, with a simple definite programme, at the psychological moment when the nation was a little ashamed of having bestowed so much sentiment on Negroes, and was concentrating its energies on Dollars. His programme of industrial education, conciliation of the South, and submission and silence as to civil and political rights, was not wholly original. . . . But Mr. Washington first indissolubly linked these things; he put enthusiasm, unlimited energy, and perfect faith into this programme, and changed it from a by-path into a veritable Way of Life. And the tale of the methods by which he did this is a fascinating study of human life.

It startled the nation to hear a Negro advocating such a programme after many decades of bitter complaint; it startled and won the applause of the South, it interested and won the admiration of the North; and

[31] W. E. Burghardt Du Bois, "Of Mr. Booker T. Washington and Others," in *The Souls of Black Folk* (Chicago, 1903), pp. 41–45, 50–59. There are two good biographies of Du Bois: Francis L. Broderick, *W. E. B. Du Bois: Negro Leader in a Time of Crisis* (Stanford, 1959); and Elliott M. Rudwick, *W. E. B. Du Bois: A Study in Minority Group Leadership* (Philadelphia, 1960).

after a confused murmur of protest, it silenced if it did not convert the Negroes themselves.

To gain the sympathy and cooperation of the various elements comprising the white South was Mr. Washington's first task; and this, at the time Tuskegee was founded, seemed, for a black man, well-nigh impossible. And yet ten years later it was done in the word spoken at Atlanta: "In all things purely social we can be as separate as the five fingers, and yet one as the hand in all things essential to mutual progress." This "Atlanta Compromise" is by all odds the most notable thing in Mr. Washington's career. The South interpreted it in different ways: the radicals received it as a complete surrender of the demand for civil and political equality; the conservatives, as a generously conceived working basis for mutual understanding. So both approved it, and to-day its author is certainly the most distinguished Southerner since Jefferson Davis, and the one with the largest personal following.

Next to this achievement comes Mr. Washington's work in gaining place and consideration in the North. Others less shrewd and tactful had formerly essayed to sit on these two stools and had fallen between them; but as Mr. Washington knew the heart of the South from birth and training, so by singular insight he intuitively grasped the spirit of the age which was dominating the North. And so thoroughly did he learn the speech and thought of triumphant commercialism, and the ideals of material prosperity, that the picture of a lone black boy poring over a French grammar amid the weeds and dirt of a neglected home soon seemed to him the acme of absurdities. One wonders what Socrates and St. Francis of Assisi would say to this.

And yet this very singleness of vision and thorough oneness with his age is a mark of the successful man. It is as though Nature must needs make man narrow in order to give them force. So Mr. Washington's cult has gained unquestioning followers, his work has wonderfully prospered, his friends are legion, and his enemies are confounded. To-day he stands as the one recognized spokesman of his ten million fellows, and one of the most notable figures in a nation of seventy millions. One hesitates, therefore, to criticise a life which, beginning with so little, has done so much. And yet the time is come when one may speak in all sincerity and utter courtesy of the mistakes and shortcomings of Mr. Washington's career, as well as of his triumphs, without being thought captious or envious, and without forgetting that it is easier to do ill than well in the world. . . .

Among his own people, . . . Mr. Washington has encountered the strongest and most lasting opposition, amounting at times to bitterness, and even to-day continuing strong and insistent even though largely silenced in outward expression by the public opinion of the nation. Some of this opposition is, of course, mere envy; the disappointment of displaced demagogues and the spite of narrow minds. But aside from this, there is among educated and thoughtful colored men in all parts of the land a feeling of deep regret, sorrow, and apprehension at the wide currency and ascendancy which some of Mr. Washington's theories have gained. . . .

The hushing of the criticism of honest opponents is a dangerous thing. . . . Honest and earnest criticism from those whose interests are most nearly touched,—criticism of writers by readers, of government by those governed, of leaders by those led,—this is the soul of democracy. . . .

Mr. Washington represents in Negro thought the old attitude of adjustment and submission; but adjustment at such a peculiar time as to make his programme unique. This is an age of unusual economic development, and Mr. Washington's programme naturally takes an economic cast, becoming a gospel of Work and Money to such an extent as apparently almost completely to overshadow the higher aims of life. Moreover, this is an age when the more advanced races are coming in closer contact with the less developed races, and the race-feeling is therefore intensified; and Mr. Washington's programme practically accepts the alleged inferiority of the Negro races. Again, in our own land, the reaction from the sentiment of war time has given impetus to race-prejudice against Negroes, and Mr. Washington withdraws many of the high demands of Negroes as men and American citizens. In other periods of intensified prejudice all the Negro's tendency to self-assertion has been called forth; at this period a policy of submission is advocated. In the history of nearly all other races and peoples the doctrine preached at such crises has been that manly self-respect is worth more than lands and houses, and that a people who voluntarily surrender such respect, or cease striving for it, are not worth civilizing.

In answer to this, it has been claimed that the Negro can survive only through submission. Mr. Washington distinctly asks that black people give up, at least for the present, three things,—

First, political power,

Second, insistence on civil rights,

Third, higher education of Negro youth,—and concentrate all their energies on industrial education, the accumulation of wealth, and the conciliation of the South. . . . As a result of this tender of the palm-branch, what has been the return? In these years there have occurred:

1. The disfranchisement of the Negro.

2. The legal creation of a distinct status of civil inferiority for the Negro.

3. The steady withdrawal of aid from institutions for the higher training of the Negro.

These movements are not, to be sure, direct results of Mr. Washington's teachings; but his propaganda has, without a shadow of doubt, helped their speedier accomplishment. The question then comes: Is it possible, and probable, that nine millions of men can make effective progress in economic lines if they are deprived of political rights, made a servile caste, and allowed only the most meagre chance for developing their exceptional men? If history and reason give any distinct answer to these questions, it is an emphatic *No.* And Mr. Washington thus faces the triple paradox of his career:

1. He is striving nobly to make Negro artisans, business men and property-owners; but it is utterly impossible, under modern competitive methods, for workingmen and property-owners to defend their rights and exist without the right of suffrage.

2. He insists on thrift and self-respect, but at the same time counsels a silent submission to civic inferiority such as is bound to sap the manhood of any race in the long run.

3. He advocates common-school and industrial training, and depreciates institutions of higher learning; but neither the Negro common-schools, nor Tuskegee itself, could remain open a day were it not for teachers trained in Negro colleges, or trained by their graduates. . . .

In failing . . . to state plainly and unequivocally the legitimate demands of their people, even at the cost of opposing an honored leader, the thinking classes of American Negroes would shirk a heavy responsibility. . . . It is wrong to encourage a man or a people in evil-doing; it is wrong to aid and abet a national crime simply because it is unpopular not to do so. . . . We have no right to sit silently by while the inevitable seeds are sown for a harvest of disaster to our children, black and white. . . .

It would be unjust to Mr. Washington not to acknowledge that in several instances he has opposed movements in the South which were unjust to the Negro. . . . Notwithstanding this, it is equally true to assert that on the whole the distinct impression left by Mr. Washington's propaganda is, first, that the South is justified in its present attitude toward the Negro because of the Negro's degradation; secondly, that the prime cause of the Negro's failure to rise more quickly is his wrong education in the past; and, thirdly, that his future rise depends primarily on his own efforts. . . .

His doctrine has tended to make the whites, North and South, shift the burden of the Negro problem to the Negro's shoulders and stand aside as critical and rather pessimistic spectators; when in fact the burden belongs to the nation, and the hands of none of us are clean if we bend not our energies to righting these great wrongs.

The South ought to be led, by candid and honest criticism, to assert her better self and do her full duty to the race she has cruelly wronged and is still wronging. The North—her co-partner in guilt—cannot salve her conscience by plastering it with gold. We cannot settle this problem by diplomacy and suaveness, by "policy" alone. . . .

The black men of America have a duty to perform, a duty stern and delicate,—a forward movement to oppose a part of the work of their greatest leader. So far as Mr. Washington preaches Thrift, Patience, and Industrial Training for the masses, we must hold up his hands and strive with him, rejoicing in his honors and glorying in the strength of this Joshua called of God and of man to lead the headless host. But so far as Mr. Washington apologizes for injustice, North or South, does not rightly value the privilege and duty of voting, belittles the emasculating effects of caste distinctions, and opposes the higher training and ambition of our brighter minds,—so far as he, the South, or the Nation, does this,—we must unceasingly and firmly oppose them.

My Early Relations with Booker T. Washington [32]

Since the controversy between myself and Mr. Washington has become historic, it deserves more careful statement than it has had hitherto, both as to the matters and the motives involved. There was first of all the ideological controversy. I believed in the higher education of a Talented Tenth who through their knowledge of modern culture could guide the American Negro into a higher civilization. . . . Mr. Washington, on the other hand . . . proposed to put the

---

[32] "My Early Relations with Booker T. Washington," *Dusk of Dawn: An Essay Toward an Autobiography of a Race Concept* (New York, 1940), pp. 70–80. Reprinted by permission of Harcourt, Brace & World, Inc.

emphasis at present upon training in the skilled trades and encouragement in industry and common labor.

These two theories of Negro progress were not absolutely contradictory. . . .

But beyond this difference of ideal lay another and more bitter and insistent controversy. This started with the rise at Tuskegee Institute, and centering around Booker T. Washington, of what I may call the Tuskegee Machine. Of its existence and work, little has ever been said and almost nothing written. . . .

There was no question of Booker T. Washington's undisputed leadership of the ten million Negroes in America, a leadership recognized gladly by the whites and conceded by most of the Negroes.

But there were discrepancies and paradoxes in this leadership. It did not seem fair, for instance, that on the one hand Mr. Washington should decry political activities among Negroes, and on the other hand dictate Negro political objectives from Tuskegee. At a time when Negro civil rights called for organized and aggressive defense, he broke down that defense by advising acquiescence or at least no open agitation. . . .

All this naturally aroused increasing opposition among Negroes and especially among the younger classes of educated Negroes, who were beginning to emerge here and there, especially from Northern institutions. This opposition began to become vocal in 1901 when two men, Monroe Trotter, Harvard 1895, and George Forbes, Amherst 1895, began the publication of the Boston *Guardian*. . . .

This beginning of organized opposition, together with other events, led to the growth at Tuskegee of what I have called the Tuskegee Machine. It arose first quite naturally. Not only did presidents of the United States consult Booker Washington, but governors and congressmen; philanthropists conferred with him, scholars wrote to him. Tuskegee became a vast information bureau and center of advice. . . . After a time almost no Negro institution could collect funds without the recommendation or acquiescence of Mr. Washington. Few political appointments were made anywhere in the United States without his consent. Even the careers of rising young colored men were very often determined by his advice and certainly his opposition was fatal. . . .

Moreover, it must not be forgotten that this Tuskegee Machine was not solely the idea and activity of black folk at Tuskegee. It was largely encouraged and given financial aid through certain white groups and individuals in the North. This Northern group had clear objectives. They were capitalists and employers and yet in most cases sons, relatives, or friends of the abolitionists who had sent teachers into the new Negro South after the war. These younger men believed that the Negro problem could not remain a matter of philanthropy. It must be a matter of business. These Negroes were not to be encouraged as voters in the new democracy, nor were they to be left at the mercy of the reactionary South. They were good laborers and they might be better. They could become a strong labor force and properly guided they would restrain the unbridled demands of white labor, born of the Northern labor unions and now spreading to the South. . . .

Contrary to most opinion, the controversy as it developed was not entirely against Mr. Washington's ideas, but became the insistence upon the right of other Negroes to have and express their ideas. Things came to such a pass that when any Negro complained or advocated a course of action, he was silenced with the remark that Mr. Washington did not agree with this. Naturally the bumptious, irritated, young black intelligentsia of the day declared, "I don't care a damn what Booker Washington thinks! This is what I think, and *I have a right to think.*"

It was this point, and not merely disagreement with Mr. Washington's plans, that brought eventually violent outbreak. . . .

When the *Guardian* began to increase in influence, determined effort was made to build up a Negro press for Tuskegee. . . . A number of talented "ghost writers," black and white, took service under Tuskegee, and books and articles poured out of the institution. . . . Tuskegee became the capital of the Negro nation. Negro newspapers were influenced and finally the oldest and largest was bought by white friends of Tuskegee. Most of the other papers found it to their advantage certainly not to oppose Mr. Washington, even if they did not wholly agree with him. Negroes who sought high positions groveled for his favor.

I was greatly disturbed at this time, not because I was in absolute opposition to the things that Mr. Washington was advocating, but because I was strongly in favor of more open agitation against wrongs and above all I resented the practical buying up of the Negro press and choking off of even mild and reasonable opposition to Mr. Washington in both the Negro press and the white.

PART THREE

BOOKER T. WASHINGTON IN HISTORY

Since Washington's death in 1915 numerous writers have attempted to analyze and evaluate his ideology and his role as a race leader. The following selections represent a broad range of interpretation. The first one, by Carter G. Woodson, was published only six years after Washington's death; the final one, by Louis R. Harlan, in 1966. Most of the writers emphasize the limitations which the times and circumstances in which he lived imposed upon Washington as well as the congruity between his doctrines and the dominant white opinion of his age. Merle Curti points out that Washington's ideology was more American than racial. Gunnar Myrdal praises Washington's political skill but questions his long-range statesmanship as a race leader. Rebecca Chalmers Roberts presents a psychological analysis of Up From Slavery, pointing out what the book reveals and conceals about Washington's personality.

Most of the selections, based upon Washington's published writings and speeches, are of interest as interpretations but add little to factual information about the Tuskegeean's career. Some of the more recent writers have done research in the unpublished correspondence in the Booker T. Washington Papers in the Library of Congress. Basil Mathews and Vann Woodward had some familiarity with these materials. But the work of August Meier is of special significance. Through his exhaustive study of the unpublished correspondence, he has brought to light many hitherto unknown facts about Washington's role in relation to civil rights and politics and has shown him to be a much more complex individual than the man revealed in the speeches and published writings. Louis R. Harlan, who has been engaged in intensive research in preparation for a definitive biography, has also contributed significant new facts regarding Washington's far-flung activities and influence.

Carter G. Woodson[1]

While the migrating Negroes of intelligence hid their lights under a bushel in the North, the illiterate Negroes in the South in need of their assistance in education and enterprise, too often fell into the hands of the harpies and sharks, many of whom had the assistance of unscrupulous Negroes in plundering these unfortunates.

There came forward then a Negro with a new idea. He said to his race: "Cast down your buckets where you are." In other words, the Negroes must work out their salvation in the South. . . . Seeing that the need of the Negro was a foundation in things economic, he came forward with the bold advocacy of industrial education of the Negroes "in those arts and crafts in which they are now employed and in which they must exhibit greater efficiency if they are to compete with white men." The world had heard this before, but never had an educator so expounded this doctrine as to move the millions. This man was Booker T. Washington.

The celebrated pronunciamento of Washington was set forth in his address at the Atlanta Exposition in 1895, and his educational theory and practice have not since ceased to be a universal topic. He insisted that since Negroes had to toil they should be taught to toil skillfully. He did not openly attack higher education for Negroes but insisted that in getting an education they should be sure to get some of that which they could use. In other words, the only education worth while is that which reacts in one's own life in his peculiar situation. . . .

Washington's plan was received by the white people in the South as a safe means by which they could promote Negro education along lines different from those followed in the education of the white man, so as to make education mean one thing for the whites and another for the Negroes. . . . The wealthy class of whites in the North took the position that there was much wisdom in Washington's policy, and with the encouragement they have given his industrial program, with

[1] Carter G. Woodson, *The Negro in Our History* (Washington, D.C., 1922), pp. 274–79. Copyright © 1922 by Associated Publishers. Reprinted by permission of Associated Publishers. Woodson founded the National Association for the Study of Negro Life and History and the *Journal of Negro History* as well as writing numerous books on Negro history.

the millions with which they have endowed Tuskegee and Hampton, and the support given the many other schools established on that basis, they, in less than a generation, have brought most northern people around to their way of thinking.

The Negroes, however, with the exception of a small minority, regarded this policy as a policy of surrender to the oppressors who desired to reduce the whole race to menial service, and they proceeded militantly to attack Washington, branding him with the opprobrium of a traitor to his people. In the course of time, however, when the South, following the advice and example of Washington, reconstructed its educational system for Negroes and began to supply these schools with faculties recommended by men interested in industrial education and too often by Washington himself, there were gradually elevated to leadership many Negroes who, in standing for industrial education, largely increased the support of Washington among his people. When, moreover, his influence as educator extended into all ramifications of life, even into politics, to the extent that he dictated the rise and fall of all Negroes occupying positions subject to the will of the whites, that constituency was so generally increased that before he died there were few Negroes who dared criticize him in public or let it be known that they were not in sympathy with his work. . . .

Washington's long silence as to the rights of the Negro, however, did not necessarily mean that he was in favor of the oppression of the race. He was aware of the fact that the mere agitation for political rights could not at that time be of much benefit to the race, and that their economic improvement, a thing fundamental in real progress, could easily be promoted without incurring the disapproval of the discordant elements in the South. He may be justly criticized for permitting himself to be drawn into certain entanglements in which he of necessity had to make some blunders. As an educator, however, he stands out as the greatest of all Americans, the only man in the Western Hemisphere who has succeeded in effecting a revolution in education. A few centuries hence, when this country becomes sufficiently civilized to stand the truth about the Negro, history will record that Booker T. Washington, in trying to elevate his oppressed people, so admirably connected education with the practical things of life that he effected such a reform in the education of the world as to place himself in the class with Pestalozzi, Froebel and Herbart.

Horace M. Bond[2]

It has often been said of Washington that he was the mouthpiece, not so much of his own race, as of the whites who looked more liberally toward a solution for the problem of the South and the Nation. There is a modicum of truth in the statement. Washington never could have attained the position which was his at the time of his death—never could have appeared to so large a proportion of his own people as the apostle of their salvation, had he not gained, early in his career, the confidence of the white people of both sections. . . . The striking personality which was his main source of strength, perhaps in a greater degree even than his sincere and honest intellect, found its expression along those avenues opened up by association and agreement with the views of his white contemporaries.

And if we are justified in saying that the relations which Washington sustained to his white associates and confreres were responsible for the degree of authority with which he appealed to his people, it is at the same time true that they were responsible for a considerable amount of the distrust and suspicion with which Washington was viewed by Negroes of the opposition school—the men who regarded the program of industrial training and the manual arts with contempt. Washington was seen by this group as the Judas of his race, who for mere popularity and power had betrayed his people to those who had previously enslaved them. . . .

Washington could assume the position of leader because he reached the Negro masses effectively. His name was the synonym of achievement throughout the "black belt." Pulpits were occupied by men whose education and training were out of tune with the sentiments echoed in the writings of DuBois and others, and as a result they turned a deaf ear to the cry of revolt and depended upon Washington for their theme. . . .

As the direct result of this control of the facilities then existent for obtaining wide publicity, the message of Washington was heard and accepted throughout the South. It must also be emphasized that

[2] Horace M. Bond, "Negro Leadership Since Washington," *South Atlantic Quarterly*, XXIV (April, 1925), 115–30. Copyrighted by the Duke University Press. Reprinted by permission of *South Atlantic Quarterly* and the author.

Washington never could have monopolized so effectually Negro leadership had not the masses of Negroes been confined to the South. . . .

Negro intellectuals had no such media as Washington for reaching the masses.

The death of this great man—we speak advisedly in so addressing him—left what might be called the industrial bloc without any effective leadership around which its effort might have focused. . . .

But what of the men whom Washington had assembled around him at Tuskegee and trained to the end that they might take up the task he would eventually relinquish? One is almost tempted to conclude that the Tuskegee regime is fatal to creative genius. . . .

What a marked contrast is to be seen in that other group, equally far removed in distance and ideals, which centers around the one man who, during the life of Washington, could divide with him the honors of Negro intellectuality. DuBois has been strikingly successful in associating with himself men and women of the highest creative ability. . . .

There can be but little hesitation in regarding the same group, composed of DuBois' protégés and intimates, as the most influential and policy-determining in the race today. . . .

It is thus that we are enabled to see the actual fruition of the influence of DuBois [in the Harlem literary renaissance of the 1920's] while that of Washington seems to have fallen upon fallow and unproductive ground. One is tempted to wonder if the teachings of the two men will explain the fact. On the one hand we have the doctrine of accommodation, compromise, and economic development as opposed to political participation and cultural distractions. On the other hand we have the doctrine of revolt, of rebellion against oppression, of protest against wrongs, of unceasing demand for a rectification of the inequalities enforced by law or custom. As the result of the first, we have a sterility which is practically total; while the second school has developed a fecundity that is amazing. . . .

The development of Negro journalism is one of the most striking factors in the course of race relations in this country. . . . It is in the field of weekly publications . . . that the most striking development has come. In the days when Washington was at the height of his power and influence, there were but one or two Negro weeklies of more than local circulation. Today there are hundreds of these publications scattered throughout the country, wielding an immense amount of power in moulding the opinions of the Negro masses to which they appeal. The attitude of these papers is an anomalous one. While omitting no tithe of respect for Washington, in fact, while regarding him editorially as the most prominent Negro the race has yet produced, their program is consistently opposed to that of the Tuskegee principal, and the ideals of that institution. *The Chicago Defender,* most powerful of all Negro weeklies, is a case in kind. On certain regular occasions it reiterates the belief that Washington is the "proudest boast of the American Negro," and yet the editorial pages of this publication are replicas, in spirit and aim, of those of *The Crisis.*[3] It preaches political participation, armed resistance to any attempts at segregation or violence, and where Washington counciled [*sic*] the Negro to "let down his bucket where he was," the *Defender* carries an article every week urging migration, and a pungent cartoon illustrating the woes of the South and the promised weal of the North. Any separation in the schools, actual or proposed, meets with the wholehearted opposition of the paper, and miscegenation is openly advocated by Robert Abbott, the owner. No Negro paper would dare expose itself to the ridicule and disfavor of its patrons by espousing the kind of education which Washington considered the sole salvation of his race. Yet Tuskegee and Hampton receive loud encomiums, and the anomaly is repeated in other fashions. . . .

Thus is the situation today. In the South, there is no Negro to take up the reins and direct the race after the fashion suggested by Washington along the road toward progress and self-esteem. On the other hand, Dubois, long the rival of Washington, has at last come into his own, with recognition in the form of literary, political, and economic ideals held by the more advanced members of his group. He is the most vital and interest compelling figure in the Negro world today. And in some measure this position is due to the pioneer work of his great competitor of a decade or so ago. It is possible that it was the economic foundation laid by Washington which has made possible the success, the position, attained by Dubois since his death. . . .

In politics it seems that the Negro has departed forever from the counsel of Washington. Will this same attitude characterize the Negro in his relations with the other of the larger questions of policy which Washington advocated?

Whatever answers are proposed to these queries, one should be ex-

---

[3] *The Crisis* was the publication of the National Association for the Advancement of Colored People and was edited by W. E. B. Du Bois.

ceedingly cautious; for social factors as yet undreamed of may arise to complicate still further the final consummation. Had not the war and subsequent stoppage of immigration turned the eye of the Negro laborer to the North, there is every possibility that Washington might yet occupy the premier position of influence in the aspirations of his people; that economic salvation and industrial development, sobriety of demeanor and good behaviour [*sic*], might yet constitute the pleas of Negro leaders. . . .

Merle Curti[4]

Washington's emphasis on a practical education for the Negro is explained by his belief that, in order to break down racial prejudice and to achieve real progress for the black, the Southern white must be convinced that the education of the former slaves was in the true interest of the South—in the interest, in short, of the Southern white himself. Far from appealing to disinterested motives, this black leader believed in the efficacy of appealing to the self-interest of the dominant whites. In their hands lay the granting or withholding of funds for Negro schools. In their hands, moreover, lay the administration of court justice and the alternative device of the rope and faggot— the year after Washington arrived at Tuskegee forty-nine black men were lynched, and in 1892, ten years later, the number was 155. In the hands of the ruling race, too, lay a thousand other matters which vitally affected the blacks. It was clear to Washington that the alliance with Northern whites during Reconstruction had failed to effect any permanent guarantees to his race; and it was equally clear that the more militant and aggressive behavior of the post-war days had provoked reaction and the violence of the Ku Klux Klan. Where aggressiveness and militancy had failed, an appeal to the self-interest of the dominant whites might succeed. The founder of Tuskegee faced the facts and acted according to his light.

In his effort to enlist the sympathy and co-operation of the white community in Tuskegee Washington was surprisingly successful. His warning that white men, by holding blacks in the gutter, would have to stay there with them, was a compelling argument when it became clear that the whole community actually did profit by what was being done for the Negro. . . . When he insisted that the great majority of his race did not expect or desire social equality, he still further disarmed the whites.

The astute Negro leader also did much to dispel the bugbear of black political domination. At first he said very little about the con-

[4] Merle Curti, "The Black Man's Place: Booker T. Washington 1856?–1915," in *The Social Ideas of American Education* (New York, 1935), pp. 293–95, 298–304, 306–09. Copyright © 1935 by Charles Scribner's Sons; renewal copyright © 1963. Reprinted by permission of Charles Scribner's Sons.

stitutional right of the Negro to vote. Only very cautiously and gradually did he come to advocate the desirability of permitting educated and property-owning blacks to exercise the right of suffrage. . . .

Subsequent lectures, articles, and books consolidated the position thus won. In view of the bids that the South was making for Northern capital, it was not without significance that the Negro educator declared in the Atlanta speech, as he had done before and continued to do, that his people had never engaged in strikes or given any labor trouble. . . .

Regardless of the extent to which Washington succeeded in convincing Northern financial groups that industrial education of the Negro promised a skilled, docile, and cheap labor supply, and that racial friction would diminish, he certainly found it, after his reassuring speeches, less of a struggle to obtain endowment for his institution. Both the Peabody and Slater funds increased their subsidies; and the great railroad magnate Collis Huntington and such industrialists as Andrew Carnegie, H. H. Rogers of the Standard Oil Company, William H. Baldwin, and Robert Ogden discovered the value of the work which was being done at Tuskegee, and contributed to its exchequer. . . .

Convinced that the Negro was at his best in the country and that he showed up worst in the city, Washington made every effort to persuade his people to acquire the farms on which they lived. Yet, as the years passed, he came more and more to sympathize with the Negro business man and to reverence the business ideal of life. . . .

If the Negro business man was successful, Washington felt that then prejudice and color could not long shut the race out from a share in any of the responsibilities of the community in which they lived, or in any opportunity or position that a self-respecting people would desire to possess. . . . He sponsored the National Negro Business League and in refutation of the charge that the race was lacking in thrift, executive talent, and organizing ability, cited with pride the success of colored men in business.

The black leader was merely accepting the dominant business philosophy of his day. Like most Americans, he did not ask how fortunes were made, nor question the ethics of the captains of industry and finance. Accepting the tenet that whenever the Negro failed to find steady employment, it was due to his shiftlessness, his unreliability, and his easy-going ways, he begged his people, in heart to heart talks, to cultivate the business virtues. . . .

Believing that if the blacks knew something of the burdens borne by the masses of Europe they would realize that their own position was by no means unique or hopeless, as many had supposed, Booker T. Washington went to Europe in 1910 to study the "man farthest down." He came back with an optimistic message for his people. . . .

Although Washington found much evidence that the masses in Europe were getting ahead, he doubted whether trade unions, strikes, Socialism, and revolution could improve their lot. Wherever the governing classes had made concessions, wherever remedial measures and reforms had been granted, the spirit of revolution had subsided. While he admitted that he did not very clearly understand Socialism, he expressed doubt whether, human nature being what it was, the Socialist program could be realized in the way its adherents believed. It was the American individualist of the middle class, not the Negro, who spoke when he declared that as human capacities differed, so opportunities and rewards must also differ. As a Southerner he paid tribute to the *laissez-faire* theory that the best government was that which governed least; and as an American, he repudiated reform by revolution and by political machinery which directed and controlled the individual from the outside. Neither his own race nor the substantial friends of Tuskegee could doubt where he stood. Possibly, however, there was something of an ironical warning in his statement that the dominant class in Europe had patriotically striven to strengthen the existing order by freeing it from the defects that endangered its existence. . . .

Washington's social philosophy was, in fine, more typical of middle-class white Americans, whom he wanted his people to be like, than it was of the Negro as such. It is true that in appealing to former slaves and their offspring to eschew militancy and conflict with the whites in the effort to improve the status of the race, he capitalized the black man's way of getting along by laughing, dancing, and singing. But little was said about the qualities of gayety, humor, and wistful whimsicality, virtues and gifts which some thought might enrich and soften the driving, efficient, and machinelike ways of the American whites. On the contrary, Washington made simplicity, earnestness, frugality, and industry the great desiderata. One searches his writings in vain for any appreciation of the aesthetic and cultural values of the African background, of the "spirituals," or of the generally pleasant, easy-going ways of the black man. Although very occasionally he made a bow to the need of cultivating the beautiful, he resembled Franklin in paying much greater deference to whatever was useful and practical.

In other ways Washington was like the average American. His insistence on looking at the bright side of things, his devotion to getting ahead by self-help, his conviction that every one had his future in his own hands, that success came to him who was worthy of it, and that the greater the obstacles, the greater the victory over them—all this characterized the thought and feeling of most Americans. Equally typical of the dominant psychology of the middle and upper classes was his denial of any conflict or cleavage of interest between worker and employer, white and black. His was the gospel of class co-operation. His boast that his race had never been guilty of declaring strikes was pleasant to Americans who loved to think that there could be no justification in such disturbances to decency and public order. His patriotic belief that, however bad conditions were for his race at home, the masses of Europe were even worse off, was likewise good American doctrine. . . .

Washington's position is better understood when it is remembered that he began his work when race hatred was at its height and when emotions were strained and tense. . . .

Education of the hands helped in fact to bridge the gap between slavery and freedom; it taught thousands of Southern whites to accept Negro education, not merely as a necessary evil, but as a possible social benefit. The good will that Washington won was at least partly responsible for increasing public support to Negro colleges and schools. . . .

The industrial school was . . . realistic and not without victories in its practical object of aiding the black man to find a place in American life in which he could make a decent living as the foundation of culture. . . .

Yet . . . industrial training did not keep the Negro farm population from decreasing; it did not enable the Negro artisan to gain proportionately in industry; it did not establish Negro business on a sound footing. Leaders of the movement ignored the fact that at the very time when the crusade for industrial training was being launched, the technological basis of industry was rapidly shifting from that of the skilled artisan to machine production. They failed to see that the machine, by invading the farm, was already beginning to push even the established farmer to the wall. . . .

In view of the hostility of organized labor to the black and the general ineffectiveness of Socialism on the one hand, and the friend-liness of men of great wealth on the other, it was, of course, entirely natural for Washington to take the stand he did. Moreover, there was much justification for his emphasis on the immediate amelioration of his race within the system that actually existed. Until collaboration with the dominant class among the whites had been proved to be ineffective as an instrument for elevating the race, it was natural to pin great faith to it. . . .

If the Negro were to fit into the existing system—and what could seem more natural and desirable to a former slave?—Washington offered a realistic approach to the problem. . . . The limitations of his social thinking were not, primarily, those of a Negro—they were those of the class which, on the whole, determined American values and governed American life.

Guy B. Johnson[5]

Booker T. Washington is the only Negro leader who has ever had anything like a race-wide following. To the masses he is a typical American hero. Born in bondage, he struggled for an education, caught a vision of the need of his people, founded a humble vocational school at Tuskegee, Alabama, spread his message to white and black, and in a few years was hailed as the Moses of his people. Like many another self-made American, he believed that hard work, thrift, and honesty were rewarded with success, and he formulated the problem of the Negro in those simple terms. . . .

Strange as it may seem at first glance, Washington was in some respects a greater leader of white opinion than he was of Negro opinion. Under the circumstances it was inevitable that white sentiment would play the leading role in determining the type of Negro leadership which would succeed. Washington was a peacemaker. He reassured the white people of the South and relieved the tension which they felt on three points in particular: political participation, education, and social relations. . . .

Booker T. Washington's popularity continued undiminished until his death in 1915. In fact, it has still a remarkable vitality, especially in the South, twenty years after his death. The reason is that Washington was the symbol of a great mass sentiment—a sentiment which created him as its leader. . . .

Booker Washington's Atlanta oration was the signal for the mobilization of a countermovement. Most northern Negroes and a large but relatively inarticulate group of southern Negroes were embittered by the outcome of Reconstruction. The Negro, they thought, should insist upon his rights, should resist the tightening grip of the caste system with all his might. The rise of Booker Washington, with his conciliatory and submissive tactics, was to their way of thinking a backward movement. Thus it came about that Washington's hour of triumph was their signal to do something in an organized way to

[5] Guy B. Johnson, "Negro Racial Movements and Leadership in the United States," *American Journal of Sociology*, XLIII (July, 1937–May, 1938), 63, 65–69. Reprinted by permission of the University of Chicago Press and the author.

stir the Negro from his lethargy and make him militant in his insistence on his rights.

The ideal leader of this movement was at hand. He was W. E. B. DuBois. . . . In 1903 in his book, *The Souls of Black Folk*, DuBois's philosophy became apparent. Of Washington he said: "Booker T. Washington arose essentially the leader of not one race but two. He was a compromise between the South, the North and the Negro." . . .

The Atlanta riot of 1906, coming as it did only a few years after what DuBois was pleased to call Washington's "Atlanta Compromise," was more than his patience could bear. In 1910 he went North to take a prominent part in a new organization, the National Association for the Advancement of Colored People. From 1910 to 1934 he served as publicity director and editor of the *Crisis*, the official organ of the Association.

The N.A.A.C.P. was founded on the belief that if the Negro would organize his forces and strive for the recognition of his legal rights, he would eventually, through the exercise of those rights, particularly the suffrage, be able to take care of himself. . . .

Now, while this legalistic approach has been successful in the sense that it has sometimes served as a goad to the South and that it has won numerous important legal cases—some of them United States Supreme Court decisions involving new precedents—it is doubtful whether it has brought the Negro any nearer his goal. . . . Sociologically the weakness of the movement is inevitable and incurable: it attempts to undo the folkways and mores of the southern caste system by attacking the results and symptoms of the system. Paradoxically, if it leaves the attitudes and folkways of the white man out of its picture, it is doomed to fail; and if it takes those attitudes and folkways into account, it is either forced back to the gradualistic and conciliatory position of Booker Washington or forced forward into revolutionary tactics. . . .

Significantly, DuBois, whose name was for over twenty-five years virtually synonymous with the N.A.A.C.P., has lately broken with the organization. . . . DuBois now stands on a platform which bears striking resemblances to the platform of Booker T. Washington, and his supporters are likely to come from the ranks of southern Negroes who once considered him "radical." . . .

The economic crisis of the present decade has shown the Negro more clearly than anything else has ever done that his economic position is marginal and insecure. In despair he has shown an increasing interest in the economic interpretation of his career in America and a disposition to believe that some mighty medicine like communism is the only alternative to a permanent status of insecurity. As time goes on, and as more and more Negro thinkers become impatient with the tactics of middle-ground movements like the N.A.A.C.P., the Urban League, and the various inter-racial agencies, there will be a shift in two directions. Those whose interests and temperaments call for caution and security will become what, for want of a better term, we may call neo-Washingtonians. That is, they will combine the philosophy of Booker Washington with as much dignified militancy as is compatible with the increase in white liberalism since the days of Washington. Those whose experience and class position have caused them to lose faith in moderationist programs will find a new hope in radicalism. They will increasingly come to believe that the white and black proletariat can and will unite and solve two problems— economic and racial—with one great revolution.

W. Edward Farrison[6]

On February 2, 1895, Frederick Douglass died in Washington, D.C. For more than fifty years he had been the acknowledged leader and champion of the Negro in America. On September 18, 1895, Booker T. Washington delivered a speech at the Cotton States Exposition in Atlanta, Georgia, . . . As a result of his speech Mr. Washington at once came to be looked upon as a successor to Frederick Douglass, the "leader of the Negro people." Since then—at least until the late Dr. Robert Moton retired [7]—the presidency of Tuskegee has been considered by many as an oracle so far as the problems of Negroes are concerned. This has not been due to accident. Booker T. Washington's philosophy of education and his views as a "leader of the Negro people" were the same, and in the development of Tuskegee he endeavored to embody both.

The story of Mr. Washington's early life is typical of success stories, with the exception that the difficulties he had to overcome in order to survive, to say nothing of "succeeding" in the peculiarly American sense of the word, were unusually brutal. From his early experiences he learned to cope with practical situations of the moment without too nice a consideration of the abstract principles and questions that might be involved. When after his schooling at Hampton Institute, Mr. Washington went to work as a teacher in a South that was rapidly being unreconstructed, he found by far the majority of Negroes unlettered and poverty-stricken. To him it appeared that the immediate problems of these Negroes were more economic and personal than political—that it was, first of all, a problem of helping them to provide themselves with the concrete necessities for comfortable and wholesome family life, rather than a matter of inspiring them to strive after the ideals of citizenship, general learning, and liberal culture. . . .

Although Mr. Washington is often accredited with developing a

[6] W. Edward Farrison, "Booker T. Washington: A Study in Educational Leadership," *South Atlantic Quarterly*, XLI (July, 1942), 313–17. Copyrighted by the Duke University Press. Reprinted by permission of *South Atlantic Quarterly* and the author.

[7] Dr. Robert Moton was Washington's successor as principal of Tuskegee Institute.

new theory of education, the lessons he endeavored to teach were not new. His doctrine concerning work was essentially the same as the "gospel of labor" which Thomas Carlyle—whom he had probably not read extensively—had preached in spluttering and cryptic exclamations earlier in the nineteenth century. The lessons of economy and thrift, as everyone knows, had been promulgated in colonial America more than a hundred years before by that apostle of material comfort and progress, Benjamin Franklin—whom Mr. Washington, doubtless, had read. Moreover, Mr. Washington's teachings were of the very form and pressure of his time. Mr. Washington came forth at the time when a great many other Americans whose beginnings were unpromising, but whose opportunities were greater than his, were working diligently and shrewdly—if not always honestly—to make themselves gods of the very comfort and well-being and respectability for which Mr. Washington taught Negroes to strive. Incidentally, it may be noted that in a large measure Tuskegee was built and has thrived on the blessings of the gods of ease who during the Gilded Age enshrined themselves in temples of wealth and power. . . .

In a half a dozen books, several articles, and numerous speeches Mr. Washington reiterated his views, frequently using the same phraseology and the same examples. Here and there he pointed to individual Negroes who had succeeded by means of industrial training, thrift, and tact. What these had done, he said, Negroes as a group could do. But he seemed to overlook the fact that these isolated instances were more often the exception than the rule and, therefore, proved little or nothing about the group, hampered as it was, and still is, by crushing circumstances which individuals now and then succeed in surmounting.

Almost fifty years have passed since Mr. Washington came into prominence as an educator and leader. In spite of notable industrial progress and economic advancement and the make-believe of the over-optimistic, the masses of Negroes, especially in the South, are still living in poverty and ignorance. During the last fifty years but few of the blessings envisioned by Mr. Washington have come; and the economic and social, as well as the political problems of the masses of Negroes still remain to be solved. If time has thus belied Mr. Washington's views, it is probably due less to chance than to their inherent weaknesses.

Granted that there is moral value as well as dignity in manual labor, and that economic independence may be achieved by industrial skill—though the depression of the 1930's leads one to wonder whether any amount or kind of education or training can guarantee economic security—how can the Negro secure to himself the benefits of his labor unless he has some influence in the determination of his value to the community as a worker? And how can he have this while, because of a lack of influence and power in the body politic, he can still work only at such jobs as are *given* to him? Obviously, one who is powerless to choose his job is equally powerless to demand full reward for his labor. . . .

As a result of the promulgation of Mr. Washington's views industrial training of a kind became a feature of Negro education in the South and has remained thus ever since. . . .

Despite the increase in the number of industrial schools, however, industrial training has remained principally a verbal feature of Negro education—for reasons which one needs no philosopher's lantern to see. First, with but one or two exceptions the private schools have never been adequately equipped to offer thorough industrial training to anybody, and the one or two exceptions could accommodate only a negligible minority of those who might have profited by such training. Second, until recently, . . . probably nowhere in the South was it given anything approaching adequate support out of public funds. The fact is, the sham industrial education provided for Negroes at public expense would have been altogether farcical if it had not had so many tragic aspects. . . .

Why have matters developed thus? Not because everybody has been naive enough to believe that everything has been lovely, but because Negroes as a group have not been sufficiently influential and powerful politically to demand better consideration from those in control of public funds and public policies. The fact that the very kind of education advocated by Mr. Washington for the masses of Negroes and verbally supported by others has never really been made available demonstrates graphically one of the most palpable weaknesses in his argument. The very means—namely, industrial education, by which he taught the masses of Negroes to achieve civil and political independence is itself a part of a larger end—namely, equal educational opportunities—towards which civil and political independence is the only sure means.

Gunnar Myrdal[8]

Gunnar Myrdal characterizes Washington as "the supreme diplomat of the Negro people through a generation filled with severe trials, who was able by studied unobtrusiveness to wring so many favors from the white majority. . . ."

[In the post-Reconstruction period when the Negro was fighting a losing struggle. . . .] In this great calamity for the Negro cause, Booker T. Washington stepped forward and established himself as the national leader of a pragmatic and conciliatory school of thought, to which a great number of national and local Negro leaders, particularly in the South, adhered.

It is wrong to characterize Washington as an all-out accommodating leader. He never relinquished the right to full equality in all respects as the ultimate goal. But for the time being he was prepared to give up social and political equality, even to soft-pedal the protest against inequalities in justice. He was also willing to flatter the Southern whites and be harsh toward the Negroes—*if* the Negroes were only allowed to work undisturbed with their white friends for education and business. But neither in education nor in business did he assault the basic inequalities. In both fields he accepted the white doctrine of the Negroes' "place." In education he pleaded for vocational training, which—independent of whether or not it be judged the most advantageous direction of schooling for the Negroes—certainly comforted the whites in their beliefs about what the Negroes were good for and where they would be held in the occupational hierarchy. Washington did not insist upon the Negroes [*sic*] rights, but he wanted a measure of tolerance and some material assistance. Through thrift, skill, and industry the Negroes were gradually to improve so much that, at a later stage, the discussion could be taken up concerning his [*sic*] rights. This was Washington's philosophy. . . .

[8] Gunnar Myrdal, "The Tuskegee Compromise," in *An American Dilemma: The Negro Problem and Modern Democracy* (New York, 1944), pp. 739–41, 743. Copyright © 1944 by Harper & Row, Publishers, Inc. Reprinted by permission of Harper & Row, Publishers, Inc.

147

It is a political axiom that Negroes can never, in any period, hope to attain more *in the short-term power bargain* than the most benevolent white groups are prepared to give them. This much Washington attained. With shrewd insight, Washington took exactly as much off the Negro protest—and it had to be a big reduction—as was needed in order to get the maximum cooperation from the only two white groups in America who in this era of ideological reaction cared anything at all about the Negroes: the Northern humanitarians and philanthropists and the Southern upper class school of "parallel civilizations." Both of these liberal groups demanded appeasement above all. And *so the Southern conservatives were actually allowed to set the conditions upon which Washington and the Southern and Northern liberals could come to terms.*

But this was hardly Washington's fault. It is not proven that he could have pressed the bargain he made for the Negro people more in their favor. Remembering the grim reaction of the period, it is difficult to study his various moves without increasingly feeling that he was truly a great politician, probably the greatest one Negro people have ever had. For his time, and for the region where he worked and where then nine-tenths of all Negroes lived, his policy of abstaining from talk of rights and of "casting down your buckets where you are" was entirely realistic. Even today it is still—in local affairs where the short-range view must dominate—the only workable Negro policy in the South. . . .

It is a different question, however, if *under the long-range perspective* it was true statesmanship, or, more specifically, if it was all the statesmanship that was called for by the interests of the Negro people. The only reason why this problem needs to be raised is the fact that *Washington was not only a national leader, but actually held a virtual monopoly of national Negro leadership for several decades.* Had this not been so, it is natural that a division of responsibility would have worked itself out, so that different individuals and groups would have taken care of the long-range and short-range interests. The actual course of policy would have become the result of discussion and interaction between them. . . .

The Niagara movement represented the first organized attempt to raise the Negro protest against the great reaction after Reconstruction. Its main importance was that it brought to open conflict and wide debate two types of Negro strategy, one stressing accommodation and the other raising the Negro protest. Booker T. Washington and W. E. B. DuBois became national symbols for these two main streams of Negro thought. . . .

The agitation did not, for a long time, seriously encroach upon Booker T. Washington's power position. But he had increasingly to concede a place before the Negro public to astute critics of his conciliatory policy and to proponents of a more militant course of action. And he had to watch his own words and deeds carefully. He had, thereafter, to reckon not only with reactions from the whites but also reactions from the Negroes. As he grew older he increasingly took on symbolic dignity in his personal appearance. He also became more interested in stressing the principal demands of Negroes for ultimate equality. The irritation between the two groups remained, but when he died in 1915, he had moved considerably toward his opponents. And he knew that he no longer spoke alone for the whole Negro people. . . .

DuBois, on his side, had become prepared to accept segregation in practice if it meant greater material advantage for Negroes. For example, he accepted segregation in the Army in order to get any Negro officers among the fighting forces at all.

Rebecca Chalmers Barton[9]

There is still magic in the name of Booker T. Washington. No Negro leader can lay stronger claim to Emerson's dictum that an institution is but the lengthened shadow of a great man. The development of agricultural and vocational education for Negroes is almost synonymous with his career. It will take more than the few decades since his death to dilute the influence of his thought and conduct on Negro-white relations. Even when the student of the subject decides that the tradition is at last dead, even as he consigns it to the dustbin of historical records, he will often be amazed to discover a flicker of life.

On second thought, he accepts this phoenix-like quality of Washington's philosophy as a recurring theme in group interaction. While some will deplore his "Uncle Tom" attitudes, others will admit their popular appeal. In the experience of the Negroes it has not been easy to slough off the slave mentality instilled over a long period of years. The metamorphosis from slave to man, with all the rapid demands for adjustment this involved, necessitated experiment in various directions. Advance and retreat, rebellion and compromise naturally characterize the Negroes' attempt to wrest a new status from a dominant white group. Any method which brought lush dividends won adherents.

Therefore a consideration of twentieth-century Negro autobiography can aptly begin with Booker T. Washington's *Up From Slavery*, written in 1900. As he gathered the material for the personal history the events of his life had already assumed symbolic importance. The views he promulgated, not only educational but also economic, political, and moral, had already established a norm. His book contains the raw materials of a legend, a solid, substantial legend which throve in both life and literature. . . .

Up From Slavery has the comprehensive quality of a "cradle to the grave" account. The author assumes that an eager public wishes to

[9] Rebecca Chalmers Barton, "Up From Slavery," in *Witnesses for Freedom: Negro Americans in Autobiography* (New York, 1948), pp. 3–4, 8–16. Copyright © 1948 by Harper & Row, Publishers, Inc. Reprinted by permission of Harper & Row, Publishers, Inc.

150

know the full story of his life struggle, for he is a classic example of the self-made man, so dear to an American public, with the success story only enhanced by the added handicap of race. The title of his book sets the tone, especially if we place the emphasis on the first word. *Up* connotes all the "bloody but unbowed" progress, all the noble aspiration and strong character clinging to the log cabin tradition. . . .

Even under difficulties, Booker T. Washington writes as a humanitarian and an optimist. His moral precepts are bound together in this framework. This whole attitude towards life is preserved instead of dissolved by the acid test of the race problem. Rather than wavering into bitterness or confusion before the raw details of prejudice he seems to rise to new heights of idealism. . . .

In this spirit of bright friendliness he can hurdle the Ku Klux Klan. He refers to their cruelties in Reconstruction days, but "simply for the purpose of calling attention to the great change that has taken place. . . . Today there are no such organizations in the South, and the fact that such ever existed is almost forgotten by both races."

This best-of-all-possible-worlds motif reappears constantly. . . .

With such homely virtues, willing cooperation, and mellow philosophy, it would be strange indeed if Booker T. Washington had not been accepted even by white Southerners. But he paves the way even further for a royal welcome. He publicizes in his autobiography specific views about slavery and about the comparative traits of Negroes and whites.

In his reminiscences, cause and effect lose their sharp contours. As he looks back on his childhood, in spite of the animal-like existence he describes, he does not feel that his owners were "especially cruel"; even his unknown white father was not to blame. . . .

As a precaution against misunderstanding, he warns his readers that he is not trying to justify slavery. Again, the fact that he feels called upon to do so is revealing. Always he seems conscious of two audiences, of two sets of interests that he must try to reconcile. He must walk the razor's edge between Negro pride and white prejudice.

With this dilemma in mind, he makes an appraisal of both groups. Starting with the Negroes, we note that he speaks of them always in general and in racial terms. As a race, they are loyal; in few instances have they betrayed a "specific trust." As a race, they lack bitterness, much as they long for freedom in their patient way. As a race, they have an eager desire for education. They are by nature responsive to help: ". . . this is not more true of any race than of the Negro. Let them once understand that you are unselfishly interested in them, and you can lead them to any extent."

To his way of thinking, these characteristics are all to the good. He seems to feel that there is nothing here to offend the Negroes or to disturb the whites. So, to be truly objective, he must expose a more unfavorable side of his group.

This is accomplished with apparent ease. He pokes fun at their first foolish enthusiasms after Emancipation: their "craze for Greek and Latin learning," fondness for big titles, "desire to hold office." He bemoans the so-called educated Negro, "with a high hat, imitation gold eye-glasses, a showy walking-stick, kid gloves, fancy boots, and what not . . ." He tells anecdotes deprecating Negroid laziness and ignorance.

But what disturbs him most is the wrong set of values he observes. Money is often misused. . . . Families will have organs, sewing machines, and ornate clocks but no forks, vegetable gardens, or decent clothes.

This distorted judgment carries over to education. We are given a dismal picture of a young man studying a French grammar while sitting in a filthy one-room cabin with grease on his clothes and weeds in his garden. . . . To reduce his point to the simplest denominator, he believes that teaching the use of the toothbrush brought about "a higher degree of civilization among the students."

We can almost chart the course of approval among many whites. As he confirms their stereotypes about a childlike, irresponsible, but good-natured group he must induce a state of glowing comfort. If they are doing the Negroes as well as themselves a service by restricting them to the sphere of manual skills, how much more pleasant for all concerned.

It seems to follow logically that white Southerners are justified in withholding higher political as well as higher educational rights from a backward group. . . .

Again, Washington hastens to add that he believes in universal, free suffrage, in principle. But after all, there are "peculiar conditions that justify the protection of the ballot in many of the states, for a while at least, either by an educational test, a property test, or by both combined . . ." Since he, himself, has gone to considerable pains in his autobiography to describe the low level of Negro education and property ownership in the South, it would seem that this opinion is another and practical basis for postponing Negro enfranchisement indefinitely. . . .

Promoted by this whole complex of thought, ovations become a commonplace in the meteoric rise of Booker T. Washington. His famous speech at the Atlantic Exposition in 1895 crowns his victories. . . .

Actually, the complete text, included in his autobiography, fails to disclose a single new idea. It is only a dramatic reinforcement and expansion of his previous views on race relations. For many years he has been building up towards this particular rejection of social equality which made history. . . .

One gathers, at first, that there were no dissenting voices. No foes would feel at home in the general mood of optimism which flows from this autobiography. Yet so strong were the repercussions of this Atlanta speech that he touches upon the matter in passing. According to his interpretation, the trouble seems to lie in his "too liberal" remarks about southern whites. "For a while there was a reaction, so far as a certain element of my own race was concerned, but later these reactionary ones seemed to have been won over to my own way of believing and acting."

Such a light dismissal of historic opposition is suspicious. It forces us to digress from the autobiography long enough to mention a fact which it chooses to ignore. There were many keen-minded Negroes, especially in the North, who regarded his point of view as dangerous, as a betrayal of the race. So positive and articulate were they that they constituted a separate school of thought spearheaded by Dr. W. E. B. Du Bois. . . .

Booker T. Washington's oversimplification on this score is the clue to the whole surface nature of his personal history. This busy, self-made man has evidently had no time to understand his own motives or no inclination to share them. Often, as we read, we suddenly become aware of a kind of double talk wherein this and that are both true and not true. Outer disagreements he irons out almost before they can occur. Inner conflicts he cushions with velvet motives. Criticism of his beliefs he silences by the solid achievements of his life.

Why could he not bear the thought of friction? Why did he learn to tread so carefully between the feelings of white and colored? Why did he align himself, in the last analysis, with the powerful, the wealthy, or the majority? Some of the implications in these questions he would not grant; to others he would have only one simple answer: for the sake of my people. Compromise and tact were effective tools in winning gradual gains for his group. They were whittling down prejudice from a giant to a pygmy.

He paid no heed to the personal ambition which also goaded him. He applied himself to his duties heroically. He left no stone unturned to set a lasting example of the respectable and respected Negro. The job was almost too perfect. There was so little of the sluggard in Booker T. Washington that we cannot ignore the possible role of overcompensation in his personality. Perhaps he felt compelled to assertion constantly in order to disprove his "inferior" origin and connections. The price in energy must have been exorbitant.

If the results brought him personal glory, he is free to consider it a by-product of the cause. His very stress on self-effacement enables him to accept this gift with a clear conscience. His doctrine of sweetness and light seems to induce a type of self-hypnosis which is almost contagious. Seldom has a writer enjoyed with such equanimity his double role of martyr and hero, servant and leader, egoist and benefactor. . . .

Cloaked in an armor of personal immunity, he passes serenely along the path of racial plagues. His capacity to interpret the favorable acceptance of himself as a change for the better in American race relations suggests psychological explanations ranging from wishful thinking to struggle for status. His failure to analyze those underlying reasons for his personal triumph which nestle in the pages of his own life history suggests an "ostrich in the sand" technique. Whether inspired by fear, naiveté, or deliberate strategy, the result is satisfying to him. He is a master at accommodation to his environment. In this process the race problem becomes both the sword and the shining plume.

Taken as a personality sketch, then, the autobiography must be estimated in negative terms. It is not three-dimensional. It has too many omissions and reservations about the self. . . .

This very condemnation leads to a measure of exoneration. For it forces us, in a search for understanding, to consider the man in relation to his times. Just as surely as the social pressures of his day influenced Washington to become the champion of vocational education for Negroes, so did they prompt him to write a story of his life which would conform to the white demand for safe and sane Negroes. . . .

Undoubtedly Booker T. Washington was acclaimed as going as far as he could and not too far. His leadership was a comfort to both the white North and the white South since the one saw his persistence, industry, and moral character, and the other his modesty, good humor, and Christian helpfulness. One welcomed the tremendous boom he gave to Negro education, and the other drew a sigh of relief that his goals were so useful and limited. Both could shake hands over him. . . .

That he might sometimes have had his tongue in his cheek about some aspects of the fine white world seems likely, but he was too disciplined to show it.

Thus in two ways can we explain the paucity of his autobiography. The internal evidence reveals a man who apparently has little self-knowledge. His drive for power has had such a satisfying outlet in race leadership that he lives for the cause as an idealist. He rejoices in setting an example and sacrificing for his group while discounting his pleasure in recognition.

On the other hand, the external evidence indicates that he deliberately selected a role to play with the white world. Naive he may have been about understanding the deep, mysterious works of human motivation, but not about the techniques of manipulating white public opinion. . . .

Each page seems to be tempered to his white audience. Conscious suppression of the unpleasant side of intergroup life, no matter how important for public sentiment, could only result in stilted and superficial writing. Ironically enough, his expediency undermines the very concept of happy and healthy race relations which it constructs.

C. Vann Woodward[10]

It was an ex-slave who eventually framed the *modus vivendi* of race relations in the New South. Booker T. Washington was more than the leader of his race. He was also a leader of white opinion with a national following, and he propounded not merely an educational theory but a social philosophy. The historical stage was set for the entrance of this remarkable man. It was a time when the hope born of Reconstruction had all but died for the Negro, when disfranchisement blocked his political advance and the caste system closed the door to integration in the white world, when the North had abandoned him to the South and the South was yielding to the clamor of her extremists. The defiant spirit of the old Negro leaders of emancipation and Reconstruction appeared increasingly quixotic under these circumstances. . . .

The power this man came to wield over the destinies of his race and over the New South stood in striking contrast to his incorrigible humility. The man who abjured "social equality" in the South moved in circles of the elite in the North and aristocracy abroad that were opened to extremely few Southern whites. The man who disparaged the importance of political power for his race came to exercise political power such as few if any Southern white men of his time enjoyed. A sampling of his vast correspondence indicates the extent of this power. As chief patronage referee in the South for Federal appointments during the administrations of Roosevelt and Taft, he was consulted on virtually all Negro appointments and on the merits of many Southern whites. . . .

During the two decades from 1895 to Washington's death in 1915, Negro thought and policy in matters of race relations, labor, education, and business enterprise conformed in large measure to the Tuskegee philosophy. This was not due so much to the genius and personal influence of Booker Washington as to the remarkable congeniality between his doctrines and the dominant forces of his age

[10] C. Vann Woodward, *Origins of the New South 1877–1913* (Baton Rouge, 1951), pp. 356–57, 359–60, 367. Copyright © 1951 by Louisiana State University Press and the Littlefield Fund for Southern History of the University of Texas, and reprinted with their permission.

and society, forces that found an eloquent voice in the brown orator, but that would have made themselves felt in any case. Negro labor history illustrates the tendency. . . .

Booker Washington was certainly not responsible for the Negro's diminishing position in the crafts, his exclusion from unions, and his employment as a strikebreaker. Finding Negro labor in this plight, he plotted what seemed to him the most practical course. "The Negro is not given to 'strikes,' " he said. "His policy is to leave each individual free to work when, where, and for whom he pleases." He pronounced trade unionism "that form of slavery which prevents a man from selling his labor to whom he pleases on account of his color." The Negro worker should rely not upon collective bargaining but upon the paternalism of well-disposed employers. "You should remember," he reminded Southern industrialists, "that you are in debt to the black man for furnishing you with labor that is almost a stranger to strikes." . . .

The enormous vogue that industrial education enjoyed among Negro educators in the South and the extent to which the older institutions, some of them without enthusiasm, fell in with the movement are to be explained to some degree by the influence that Washington exercised over the distribution of Northern philanthropic funds. There is considerable evidence to support the view of an unfriendly critic that Washington's influence became so powerful that "almost no Negro institution could collect funds without the recommendation or acquiescence of Mr. Washington. . . ."

The shortcomings of the Atlanta Compromise, whether in education, labor, or business, were the shortcomings of a philosophy that dealt with the present in terms of the past. Not that a certain realism was lacking in the Washington approach. It is indeed hard to see how he could have preached or his people practiced a radically different philosophy in his time and place. The fact remains that Washington's training school, and the many schools he inspired, taught crafts and attitudes more congenial to the premachine age than to the twentieth century; that his labor doctrine was a compound of individualism, paternalism, and antiunionism in an age of collective labor action; and that his business philosophy was an anachronism. It is hardly necessary to add that white leaders of the South adhered pretty generally to the same doctrines and that the larger part of them subscribed to Washington's race policy.

Oliver C. Cox[11]

        Perhaps no leader among Negroes has been so unfathomable and controversial a figure as Booker T. Washington. And yet few if any studies on the Negro in the United States have been able to avoid some sort of inquiry into the nature of his leadership. We shall attempt here to present a specific typology of his role. . . .

It is necessary first to define Negro leader—to distinguish him from those who merely have achieved eminence in given fields of endeavor. . . . Thus a genuine leader among Negroes may be considered as one who takes up the common cause of the Negro people and makes a significant appeal to them to follow his program in the resolution of that cause. . . .

The collaborator is an active advocate of the purposes of the dominant group. He has to be exceedingly versed in subleties because, although he is fundamentally antagonistic to the people's cause, he must appear to be their champion. . . .

The collaborator, of course, cannot be in conflict with the dominant power, for his significance as a leader depends entirely upon that power. . . . Since the collaborator's program and advocacy is [sic] essentially that of the ruling class, he is protected from failure. He is not only given wide publicity as a phenomenal leader but also made an *intercessor* between his group and the dominant class. . . .

Besides the social situation the personality and immediate interest of the leader should be taken into account. On the pre-Civil War plantation talented black men tended to become principally either discontented bondsmen with ideas of escape and revolt, or trusted slaves. Washington's slavery experience seems to have conditioned him to the latter type of personality. . . . As a slave he would most likely have been a capital danger to such exploits as those of Harriet Tubman. . . . The favorite slave was frequently very firm in dealing with the rank-and-file of his class for being remiss in their duties. Indeed one feels constantly that Washington never fully lost the attitude of the favorite slave.

[11] Oliver C. Cox, "The Leadership of Booker T. Washington," *Social Forces*, XXX (October, 1951), 91, 94–96. Reprinted by permission of the University of North Carolina Press.

In freedom, however, he was very ambitious. His fervid aspiration to build an educational institution comparable to that of his alma mater presented him with certain material necessities which only persons of wealth could satisfy. Thus the financing of his project and the arrangement of a financially secure life for himself provided the essential *quid pro quo* in his collaboration. . . .

Washington's leadership, therefore, should be thought of as spurious. He was not a leader of the masses in the Garvian sense;[12] his function was rather that of controlling the masses. He deflated and abandoned their common cause. . . .

It has been commonly averred that Washington's leadership may be "justified" if his "times" are taken into consideration. By a like assumption, however, the manner of action of virtually all persons and all things may be explained away. . . .

Although Washington functioned as a restraint upon the Negroes' democratic progress, he still embodied some residual value. The propaganda which exalted him, his friendship with powerful members of the ruling class, and the honor which it frequently conferred upon him became a heartening symbol to the Negro people. . . .

There is a certain very simple but to many persons quite pertinent question as to whether the Negro people would have been "better off" without Washington. It may be possible to weigh this question. In the first place the Negro people never really followed Washington, for he did not lead but rather sought to divert them. The common cause of the Negro before, during, and after Washington's ascent remains the acquisition of full civil rights. This cause was seriously obscured by the pressures of the larger interests which brought Washington himself into use. . . .

Leaders of Washington's type are exceedingly serviceable to the southern ruling class. They are vastly more effective than white spokesmen in controverting the movement for democracy among Negroes. Against white workers to the latter end they are an almost complete answer, for it is assumed that no white liberal could be more interested in the Negro's welfare than the Negro himself.

[12] Marcus Garvey, a native of Jamaica, came to the United States in 1916 and organized the U.N.I.A.—the United Negro Improvement Association—which advocated black nationalism and a back-to-Africa movement. The Garvey movement is considered by many historians to have been the first genuine mass Negro Movement in the United States.

Langston Hughes[13]

Washington was in many ways a distinguished personality, provincially wise, astute, and certainly diplomatic. . . .

He was called "the leader of his people" and so billed on the national scene. But the mantle of his leadership was bestowed upon him by white America. To Negroes Booker T. Washington was for a quarter of a century a famous man, a distinguished speaker, often a front page celebrity, but never in any sense their leader in the way that Martin Luther King became a leader, inspiring hope, passion and intense devotion in a wide following. For Negroes, what Mr. Washington inspired was respect in many, mixed admiration in some, skepticism in others, and downright hatred in certain segments of the black population that refused to consider his oratorial and tactical compromises in the racial field the better part of wisdom. . . .

Historical and contemporary judgments affirm that Washington was in reality "a great accommodator." But to create Tuskegee in Alabama in that era he could hardly have been otherwise. He *did* create Tuskegee—a splendid achievement—but, in so doing, he was in turn almost forced to create of himself an image of national leadership. But in time he grew to like this image and eventually to take advantage of it, so his enemies claimed, for the exercise of power itself. As a bridge between the white and colored peoples of the United States, he sought and gained more often than not the favors of the white power structure from which came the endowments supporting Tuskegee. And before he died, the white millionaire, Andrew Carnegie, gave him and his family an income for life. . . .

The South and its Negroes at the end of Reconstruction needed a man like Booker T. Washington. ONWARD AND UPWARD was the slogan on one of the popular Booker T. Washington calendars. A glowing photograph of Dr. Washington adorned the top center crowning a pathway to the sunup [to] which freed Negroes marched with the humble tools of agriculture and simple industry in hand— hoes, mallets, axes, and hammers—while amiable and approving

[13] Langston Hughes, Introduction, *Up From Slavery* (New York, 1965), pp. v, vii–x. Reprinted by permission of Dodd, Mead & Co. Hughes was probably the best-known Negro American poet and playwright of the twentieth century.

160

whites looked on from the sidelines. Everybody seemed happy. At the top was the word PROGRESS.

This calendar decorated numerous Negro homes, barber shops, pool halls, and juke joints, but many Afro-Americans who looked upon it did not believe its message. In Alabama itself there were too many night riders in Klan hoods, too many closed ballot boxes, and too much fear. But Washington felt that these unpleasant problems would be solved gradually. "It is at the bottom of life we must begin and not the top. Nor should we permit our grievances to overshadow our opportunities. . . . The wisest among my race understand that agitation of questions of social equality is the extremest folly." As to voting rights, they would be a "slow natural growth," therefore the Negro should "deport himself modestly in regard to political claims." The South should not be forced "to do something which it did not want to do," Washington contended, since there were "peculiar conditions that justify the protection of the ballot in many of the states, for a while at least, either by an education test, a property test, or by both combined." . . .

A young New England black man, William Edward Burghardt DuBois, a scholar in the social sciences with a Harvard and European background, did not believe a word of this. DuBois, then teaching at Atlanta University, began early in his career to cross swords with Dr. Washington. He disputed the thesis that it was possible to instill in black men self respect without at the same time instilling in them the need for complete equal rights, civil, social, and political. A voteless man, no matter how well skilled he might become in agriculture, blacksmithing or tailoring as taught at Tuskegee, would remain a powerless man. . . .

A half century later during the decade following the historic Supreme Court decrees of 1954 concerning Negro education, these problems with which DuBois concerned himself exploded into even greater problems from Washington, D.C. itself to Selma, Alabama, only a stone's throw from Tuskegee. Booker Washington's great Institute had become a success, but his program of racial compromise in the South had completely and clearly failed. In 1965 the students of Tuskegee itself were picketing the Alabama State Capitol at Montgomery on behalf of the simple right to vote.

August Meier[14]

        It should not be surprising that in a period of increasing racial integration and of growing recognition of the Negro's constitutional rights, the centennial of Booker T. Washington's birth in April 1956 should have passed relatively unnoticed. For Washington was associated with a policy of compromise and conciliation toward the white South that is not in keeping with the trend of our times. Yet Washington's own correspondence reveals such extensive efforts against segregation and disfranchisement that a re-evaluation of his philosophy and activities is in order.

  Undoubtedly in reading Washington's books, articles, and speeches, one is most strongly impressed with the accommodating tone he adopted toward the white South. He minimized the extent of race prejudice and discrimination, criticized the airing of Negro grievances, opposed "social equality," accepted segregation and the "separate but equal" doctrine, depreciated political activity, favored property and educational qualifications for the franchise (fairly applied to both races), largely blamed Negroes themselves for their unfortunate condition, and counselled economic accumulation and the cultivation of Christian character as the best ways to advance the status of Negroes in American society. His ultimate ends were stated so vaguely and ambiguously that Southern whites mistook his short-range objectives for his long-range goals, although his Negro supporters understood that through tact and indirection he hoped to secure the good will of the white man and the eventual recognition of the constitutional rights of American Negroes.

  Now, although overtly Washington minimized the importance of political and civil rights, covertly he was deeply involved in political affairs and in efforts to prevent disfranchisement and other forms of discrimination. For example, Washington lobbied against the Hardwick disfranchising bill in Georgia in 1899. While he permitted whites to think that he accepted disfranchisement, he tried to keep Negroes believing otherwise. In 1903 when Atlanta editor Clark Howell

[14] August Meier, "Toward a Reinterpretation of Booker T. Washington," *Journal of Southern History*, XXIII (1957), 220–27. Reprinted by permission of the *Journal of Southern History* and the author.

implied that Washington opposed Negro officeholding, the Tuskegeean did not openly contradict him, but asked T. Thomas Fortune
of the leading Negro weekly, the New York *Age,* to editorialize, "We
are quite sure that the Hon. Howell has no ground . . . for his attempt to place Mr. Washington in such a position, as it is well understood that he, while from the first deprecating the Negro's making
political agitation and office-holding the most prominent and fundamental part of his career, has not gone any farther."

Again, while Washington seemed to approve of the disfranchisement amendments when he said that "every revised constitution
throughout the Southern States has put a premium upon intelligence,
ownership of property, thrift and character," he was nevertheless
secretly engaged in attacking them by legal action. As early as 1900
he was asking certain philanthropists for money to fight the electoral
provisions of the Louisiana constitution. Subsequently he worked
secretly through the financial secretary of the Afro-American Council's
legal bureau, personally spending a great deal of money and energy
fighting the Louisiana test case. At the time of the Alabama Constitutional Convention of 1901 he used his influence with important
whites in an attempt to prevent discriminatory provisions that would
apply to Negroes only. He was later deeply interested in the Alabama
test cases in 1903 and 1904. So circumspect was he in this instance
that his secretary, Emmett J. Scott, and lawyer, Wilford Smith, in
New York, corresponded about it under pseudonyms and represented
the sums of money involved in code. Washington was also interested
in efforts to prevent or undermine disfranchisement in other states.
In Maryland, where disfranchisement later failed, he had Catholic
lawyer F. L. McGhee of St. Paul approach the Catholic hierarchy in
an attempt to secure its opposition to disfranchisement, and urged
Episcopal divine George F. Bragg to use his influence among important whites. Washington contributed money generously to the
test cases and other efforts, though, except in the border states, they
did not succeed. In 1903 and 1904 he personally "spent at least four
thousand dollars in cash, out of my own pocket . . . in advancing
the rights of the black man."

Washington's political involvement went even deeper. Although he
always discreetly denied any interest in active politics, he was engaged
in patronage distribution under Roosevelt and Taft, in fighting the
lily-white Republicans, and in getting out the Negro vote for the
Republicans at national elections. He might say, "I never liked the

atmosphere of Washington. I early saw that it was impossible to build up a race of which their leaders were spending most of their time, thought, and energy in trying to get into office, or in trying to stay there after they were in," but under Roosevelt he became the arbiter of Negro appointments to federal office.

Roosevelt started consulting Washington almost as soon as he took office. The Tuskegeean's role in the appointment of Gold Democrat Thomas G. Jones to a federal judgeship in Alabama was widely publicized. Numerous letters reveal that politicians old and new were soon writing to Tuskegee for favors. Ex-congressman George H. White unsuccessfully appealed to Washington after the White House indicated that "a letter from you would greatly strengthen my chances." Secretary Scott reported that the President's assertion to one office-seeker that he would consider him only with Washington's "endorsement" had "scared these old fellows as they never have been scared before." Some of the established politicians played along and were helped along. Thus P. B. S. Pinchback, at one time acting governor of Louisiana, was favored throughout the Roosevelt and Taft administrations. In the case of J. C. Napier, Nashville lawyer and banker, Washington first turned him down as recorder of deeds for the District of Columbia and minister to Liberia, then named him as one of two possibilities for consul at Bahia, later offered him the Liberian post which Napier now refused, and finally secured for him the office of register of the Treasury. Examples of Washington's influence could be multiplied indefinitely, for a number of port collectorships and of internal revenue, receiverships of public monies in the land office, and several diplomatic posts, as well as the positions of auditor for the Navy, register of the Treasury, and recorder of deeds were at his disposal. Among his outstanding appointments were Robert H. Terrell, judge of municipal court in Washington; William H. Lewis, assistant attorney-general under Taft; and Charles W. Anderson, collector of internal revenue in New York.

Furthermore, Roosevelt sought Washington's advice on presidential messages to Congress and consulted him on most matters concerning the Negro. Every four years, also, Washington took charge of the Negro end of the Republican presidential campaign, he and his circle, especially Charles Anderson, recommending (and blackballing) campaign workers and newspaper subsidies, handling the Negro press, advising on how to deal with racial issues, and influencing prominent Negroes.

If Washington reaped the rewards of politics, he also experienced its vicissitudes. From the start he was fighting a desperate and losing battle against the lily-white Republicans in the South. His correspondence teems with material on the struggle, especially in Louisiana and Alabama, and in other states as well. As he wrote to Walter L. Cohen, chairman of the Republican state central committee of Louisiana and register of the land office in New Orleans, on October 5, 1905: "What I have attempted in Louisiana I have attempted to do in nearly every one of the Southern States, as you and others are in a position to know, and but for my action, as feeble as it was, the colored people would have been completely overthrown and the Lily Whites would have been in complete control in nearly every Southern State."

Troubles came thick and fast after Taft's inauguration. The new President did not consult Washington as much as Roosevelt had done, and Washington exercised somewhat less control over appointments. Atlanta lawyer Henry Lincoln Johnson forced Washington's appointee, J. C. Dancy, out of the office of recorder of deeds. Meanwhile, more offices were being emptied than filled as far as Negroes were concerned. For example, R. L. Smith, the only Negro with a "significant" federal office in Texas, was dropped, and Cohen, in spite of Taft's promises, failed of reappointment after a reorganization of the land office in Louisiana. Not until 1911, after persistent efforts to convince the administration of the need for some decent plums in order to retain the Negro vote, were a few significant appointments finally arranged. The most notable was that of W. H. Lewis as assistant attorney-general—the highest position held by a Negro in the Federal government up to that time.

In areas other than politics Washington also played an active behind-the-scenes role. On the Seth Carter (Texas) and Dan Rogers (Alabama) cases involving discrimination against Negroes in the matter of representation on jury panels, Washington helped with money and worked closely with lawyer Wilford Smith until their successful conclusion before the United States Supreme Court. He was interested in protecting Negro tenants, who had accidentally or in ignorance violated their contracts, from being sentenced to the chain gang. He was concerned in the Alonzo Bailey peonage case, and when the Supreme Court declared peonage illegal, confided to friends that "some of us here have been working at this case for over two years," securing the free services of "some of the best lawyers in Montgomery" and the assistance of other eminent Alabama whites.

In view of Washington's public acceptance of separate but equal transportation accommodations, his efforts against railroad segregation are of special interest. When Tennessee in effect prohibited Pullman space for Negroes by requiring that such facilities be segregated, he stepped into the breach. He worked closely with Napier in Nashville, and enlisted the aid of Atlanta leaders like W. E. B. DuBois.

This group did not succeed in discussing the matter with Robert Todd Lincoln, president of the Pullman company, in spite of the intercession of another railroad leader, William H. Baldwin, Jr. And, though Washington was anxious to start a suit, the Nashville people failed to act. In 1906, employing Howard University professor Kelly Miller and Boston lawyer Archibald Grimke as intermediaries, Washington discreetly supplied funds to pay ex-senator Henry W. Blair of New Hampshire to lobby against the Warner-Foraker amendment to the Hepburn Railway Rate Bill. This amendment, by requiring equality of accommodations in interstate travel, would have impliedly condoned segregation throughout the country, under the separate but equal doctrine. The amendment was defeated, but whether owing to Blair's lobbying or to the protests of Negro organizations is hard to say.

It is clear, then, that in spite of his placatory tone and his outward emphasis upon economic development as the solution to the race problem, Washington was surreptitiously engaged in undermining the American race system by a direct attack upon disfranchisement and segregation; that in spite of his strictures against political activity, he was a powerful politician in his own right. The picture that emerges from Washington's own correspondence is distinctly at variance with the ingratiating mask he presented to the world.

Louis R. Harlan[15]

Those who have thought of Booker T. Washington as a provincial southern American Negro, intellectually as well as geographically isolated from the rest of the world, will be surprised to find that he was substantially involved in African affairs. This involvement, however, did not require any fundamental readjustment of Washington's outlook. The Negroes' position in American society at the turn of the twentieth century was, after all, roughly analogous to that of Negroes in the African colonies. Both groups were politically disfranchised, socially subordinated, and economically exploited. . . . Washington's cooperation with white colonial authorities and promoters in Africa, likewise, was consistent with his public acceptance of most of the southern white racial practices and his partnership with American white elite groups of both North and South. He urged Negro peoples overseas as well as those in America to seek their individual and group interests within the existing political and racial order. Though Washington, abroad as at home, occasionally endorsed surreptitious attacks on the prevailing race system, his African experience illuminates his essential conservatism. He is seen, as in a tailor's mirror, from new angles but in the usual posture. Though he occasionally associated with more militant Negroes at home and overseas, he so thoroughly subscribed to the "White Man's Burden" of leadership and authority that, in seeming forgetfulness that he was Negro, he actually took up the burden himself. . . .

On the first day of the twentieth century Tuskegee's first venture into Africa began. A Hamburg freighter put ashore in the German colony of Togo three Tuskegee graduates and a faculty member, along with their teaching equipment—plows, wagons, a steam cotton gin, and a cotton press. Their dual task was to train Africans in cotton culture and to experiment with interbreeding of local and imported cotton to develop a hardy, commercially successful variety. This was one of many projects of the *Kolonial-Wirtschaftliches Komitee* (KWK), a

[15] Louis R. Harlan, "Booker T. Washington and the White Man's Burden," *American Historical Review*, LXXI (January, 1966), 441–43, 447–50, 452, 457–61, 464–65, 467. By permission of the author.

private German organization anxious to accelerate the economic exploitation of the German colonies. . . .

Through the influence of the German ambassador and the American Secretary of Agriculture, a team of KWK experts visited Tuskegee to secure expert and practical cotton farmers. "Some members of the company have certain misgivings whether your negro-planters might find some difficulties in starting and developing their work in Togo," Baron Herman of the *Komitee* wrote to Washington, "in finding the necessary authority towards the native population and in having at the same time the necessary respect towards the German government official[s] who of course would try to help them as best they could in their work." What he was really asking, though Washington may not have understood this, was whether the Tuskegeeans would accept the highly authoritarian German colonial administration. . . . Washington reassured the Baron: "I do not think in any case that there will be much if any difficulty in the men who go from here treating the German officials with proper respect. They are all kindly disposed, respectful gentlemen. I believe at the same time they will secure the respect and confidence of the natives." . . .

Tuskegee graduates helped to introduce cotton culture also into others parts of Africa. Some of them were employed by British promoters in Nigeria and others apparently in the Belgian Congo. More importantly, the man who opened up the fabulous cotton region of the Anglo-Egyptian Sudan chose three Tuskegee Seniors to assist him in his pioneer experimental farming in that area. Leigh Hunt, an American capitalist, acquired with British associates a large tract at Zeidab on the banks of the Nile. He brought a Tuskegee carpenter, agriculturist, and blacksmith there to organize a plantation and prepare the way for a larger colony of American Negroes. . . .

Washington's parting advice to the young men bound for the Sudan was amusingly similar to what one would expect from a Victorian parent, a warning against "going native." After reminding the boys that they had the school's reputation in their keeping, he concluded: "One point I wish to impress upon you is this, a great many persons going to a warm climate, go to ruin from a moral standpoint. I hope you will keep this in mind and remember that if you yield to the temptation and lower yourselves in your moral character, you will do yourself, the school and the race the greatest injustice; but I feel sure you are going to stand up and be men." . . .

Colonial officials in Southern Africa meanwhile sought Washington's advice on race policy. Lord Grey of the British South Africa Company, which controlled Rhodesia, suggested in a conversation with the editor William T. Stead that Washington might be employed to tour Rhodesia and report on the best methods "to raise, educate, and civilize the black man." . . . After Stead enthusiastically relayed the offer through his American colleague Albert Shaw, Washington's consideration of it was given wide newspaper publicity. He consulted with President Roosevelt and other prominent Americans and finally declined on the ground that his primary responsibility was to his institution and the American Negro, but he agreed to reconsider at a future time.

Washington was consulted also when "Milner's Kindergarten" was launching the new Union of South Africa. E. B. Sargant, appointed South African Commissioner of Education by Lord Milner, was instructed to devise a plan of education for the Orange Free State and Transvaal. His request for advice on the proper education for black Africans was forwarded to Washington by a mutual friend. Washington's answers to Sargant's questions are particularly revealing because of Washington's stated assumption that there was "no very great difference between the native problem there and the Negro problem in America." For blacks in South Africa he proposed the same accommodation, economic and cultural subordination, and incentives to individual self-help that characterized his racial philosophy in the United States. "Since the blacks are to live under the English Government," Washington wrote, "they should be taught to love and revere that government better than any other institution. To teach them this, they should receive their education and training for citizenship from or through the government. It is not always true that the Missions teach respect for the rulers in power." Washington thus supported those conservative South Africans who considered missionaries, particularly Negro American ones, as subversives. Washington also urged that the Africans be taught English in order to give them a common language and to absorb them more fully into Western culture. All should receive industrial as well as common school training, he felt, so as to "fit them to go out into this rich country and be skilled laborers in agriculture, mining and the trades." He urged that the educated class of African men be accorded civil equality with Europeans, a position that was consistent with his support of educational qualifications for suffrage in the United States. . . .

Washington became involved in a more congenial African role as defender of mistreated Negro people in King Leopold's Congo Free State. Early in the twentieth century a world-wide scandal began with the exposure of forced labor and police brutality in this supposedly model colony. Washington readily assented to the request of Thomas S. Barbour, American organizer of the Congo Reform Association, that he use his influence with high American officials in behalf of Congo reform. He called personally on his friend President Roosevelt and on members of the Senate Foreign Relations Committee to urge American diplomatic pressure on the Belgian government and monarch. . . .

It was in Liberia that Washington played his greatest African role. While his actions in this case were immediately useful, they served to support a semicolonial relationship of Liberia to the United States. During the final months of the Roosevelt administration and early in the Taft administration, when the little black republic seemed on the verge of both internal collapse and absorption by its European colonial neighbors, it was Washington who rang the fire bell, and kept ringing it. He used the leverage of the American Negro vote to engage in international as well as interracial diplomacy. This resulted in America's first serious commitment in Africa, an area far from the range of America's national interests. Washington's unofficial diplomacy in this crisis of Negro self-government illustrates the strong points of his personal style. He showed patience and mastery of detail in the untying of Gordian knots, diplomatic skill and agility developed in a lifetime of interracial negotiation, and ability to play several roles simultaneously in dealing with various groups. On the other hand, the weaknesses of Washington's approach and outlook are suggested by the nature of the American commitment in Liberia that emerged from his negotiations. Liberia became an American protectorate similar to that which had recently been imposed on the Dominican Republic. It involved an international bankers' loan and the control of customs and border police by American officials. . . .

Washington continued to influence Liberian finance, economic development, and education. While the State Department was negotiating the political settlement, Washington wrote to the banker-philanthropist Isaac N. Seligman. He asked him to "find parties in New York who would like to take up the Liberian debt, something in the way that was done in the case of San Domingo." Seligman showed interest, but it was Paul M. Warburg, a Tuskegee trustee and partner of Kuhn, Loeb and Company, who led the American banking consortium involved in the Liberian loan. Though Warburg's family firm in Germany was already interested in the loan, there is evidence that Washington also influenced his decision. In a letter to Secretary Philander C. Knox, Warburg took a philanthropic view of the loan, saying that "our associates and we hardly look upon this small transaction as a matter of business, but we rather consider it from the point of view of attempting to assist that Republic in its struggle to free itself from the oppressive influences, which are well known to you."

Washington realized that American fiscal aid was only a rescue measure for Liberia; it would do little good if economic conditions continued as before. He sought, therefore, to encourage American capital investment in Liberia. The most notable of such schemes was that of John Stevens Durham, a Philadelphia Negro, to plant sugar in Liberia on a large scale. Warburg's refusal to supply the capital brought the plan to an end. Washington also urged Liberians to accumulate their own capital by heroic measures of self-denial and enterprise. There were many things that Washington, with an outlook forged in the mid-nineteenth century, did not understand. His lifetime in the colonial economy of the American South, however, gave him a ready understanding of many of the problems of an undeveloped country such as Liberia. . . .

Washington became the best-known Negro in the world when his autobiography became a world-wide best seller. It was translated into Zulu as well as the chief European languages, and some of the Africans who corresponded with him may have done so simply because he was a celebrity. Many Africans, however, responded hopefully to his message of self-help and industrial education. Students went to Tuskegee from all over Africa, though not in large numbers because scholarships and travel funds were lacking. . . .

A curious anomaly of the Washington Papers is his friendly correspondence with most of the leaders of African nationalism. There is no evidence, however, that he encouraged or even clearly understood their nationalistic and Pan-African views. He initiated none of this correspondence, and about the only thing he seems to have had in common with the nationalists, beyond skin color, was an acquiescence in segregation, which they may have construed as similar to their desire for national separatism. . . .

A suitable culmination of Washington's long interest in Africa was the International Conference on the Negro held at Tuskegee in 1912.

The conference involved the same ambiguity of relationship to the blacks and whites that was evident in his other African activities and in his role in American society. . . . Washington hoped that it would lead to the formation of a permanent society that would be "a sort of guardian of the native peoples of Africa, a friendly power, an influence with the public and in the councils where so often, without their presence or knowledge, the destinies of the African peoples and of their territories are discussed and decided." The society should include "explorers, missionaries, and all those who are engaged, directly or indirectly, in constructive work in Africa."

Washington's formal call for the 1912 conference ignored the important but controversial issues of race and nationalism and stressed "a more systematic development of constructive educational work on the part of missionaries and governments." Invitations were sent to the leading missionary societies and to thousands of individual missionaries. The State Department at Washington's request publicized the conference among European governments that had colonial possessions in Africa or the West Indies. In view of the type of publicity, the distance from Africa, and the restrictions on travel of subject peoples, it is not surprising that most of the delegates were white. West Indians were present "in three colors," and twenty-five missionaries of twelve denominations and eighteen countries or colonies were represented, but very few black Africans.

Several influential West Africans, however, gave their blessing to the conference from a distance. . . .

A mere review of Washington's activities and expressed attitudes still leaves his role somewhat enigmatic. He never went to Africa, though he found time for three trips to Europe. He considered his principal mission in life to be the spreading of the educational system and social philosophy symbolized by Tuskegee Institute. It was consistent with this commitment to encourage American Negro enterprise and ethnocentric philanthropy in Africa. On the other hand, Washington rejected the proposals of emigrationists, visionaries, and missionaries as inconsistent with the Tuskegee ideal.

Just as Washington had built a career in the United States by telling Negroes what influential whites wanted them to hear, so in Africa he supported the principle if not all the practices of colonialism. There as here, Washington's role and outlook were complex, but they supported the concept of the white man's burden. This burden was not entirely hypocritical, of course. Washington acquiesced in the leader-ship of white men, but he was prompt to remind them when they neglected the responsibilities of power. . . . He remained a social pacifist for whom industrial education was a universal panacea. Its method and ethos seemed to him as applicable to African problems as to those of American Negroes.

Afterword

Few Americans have been awarded as distinguished posthumous honors as those conferred upon Booker T. Washington. In 1931, on the fiftieth anniversary of the founding of Tuskegee, a great bronze statue was dedicated on the Tuskegee campus as a gift from a "Committee of One Hundred Thousand Negroes." In 1940 a postage stamp bearing Washington's image was issued in a series of "Famous American Commemorative Stamps." In 1942 the S. S. "Booker T. Washington," a United States Merchant Marine Liberty Ship, was christened by Marian Anderson. In 1946 Washington was elected to the Hall of Fame, and the same year the coinage of five million Booker T. Washington half dollars was authorized by Congress. In 1948 the Booker T. Washington Birthplace, Virginia, was designated as a United States Post Office. In 1956 the birthplace was made a National Monument, and a Booker T. Washington Centennial Stamp was issued.

It is ironic that the Negro who achieved such fame and honor should have lived in a period when the legal and political rights of members of his race steadily deteriorated. It is clear today—as it was to some of his contemporaries—that Washington's great reputation during his lifetime was due largely to the fact that he preached doctrines which coincided with the prevailing beliefs and attitudes of the dominant white majority. Publicly, at least, he accepted conditions as they were and urged Negroes to make the best of adversity and not to fight against forces which they could not control. His approach to the racial situation was realistic, perhaps, but it was not heroic. Washington was a man very much in step with his times, and the heroes of history are likely to be men who are ahead of their times. Hence, in spite of the official honors bestowed upon him, the luster of his name has dimmed. The Washington story, as a story of success in the face of adversity, still has appeal, and new editions of *Up From Slavery* continue to appear, but more militant Negroes like Du Bois and Trotter have become the folk heroes of Negro Americans. A popular history by a Negro writer published in 1965 spoke of Washington as a collaborator and suggested that while he himself may not have been a "Thomist," his career paved the way for thousands of "Uncle Toms." In order to win the good will of white America, the author said, he paid too high a price and was a party to the degradation of himself and his race. The same writer praised William Monroe Trotter as "the advance man of a new breed of black rebels who fleshed out the renaissance of the Negro soul." Du Bois he characterized as "the Columbus of the Negro's New World," a man who personified the "new Negro ethos." [1]

The reasons for the decline in Washington's prestige are not hard to discern. Although he had some understanding of the times in which he lived, he had little influence on the course of events and did not foresee future developments. Negroes failed to follow his advice to remain in the South and to abjure political activity. During the First World War, almost immediately after his death, a mass exodus of Negroes from the South to northern cities began. In the North, Negroes came to exercise significant political power and were sometimes able to use their political power to wrest economic concessions, such as equal employment opportunity laws, from the dominant whites—a reversal of the Washington formula of economic foundations as the basis for political concessions. During the 1950's and 1960's the political power of northern Negroes was also a factor in bringing about the use of the authority of the federal government to protect the civil and political rights of southern Negroes for the first time since the Reconstruction era. In the South in the same period Negro leaders increasingly rejected Washington's advice and became more and more militant and politically active. The town of Tuskegee and Tuskegee Institute itself played important roles in the struggle for political rights.

As the Negro revolution of the fifties and sixties gained momentum the name of Booker T. Washington was seldom mentioned. One notable exception was the 1955 speech of Dr. Martin Luther King, Jr., which launched the Montgomery Improvement Association and King's own career as race leader. In it he mentioned Washington by name and quoted his advice: "Let no man pull you so low as to make you hate him." [2] Although King represented a repudiation of the policies of accommodation and acquiescence in segregation which Washington had come to symbolize, as a Negro leader who came out of the South, King was in some respects an heir of Washington. In his rejection of hatred and in his pleas for racial cooperation and brotherly love, he was sometimes reminiscent of the Tuskegeean.

[1] Lerone Bennett, Jr., *Confrontation: Black and White* (Chicago, 1965), pp. 106–07, 114, 116.
[2] Lerone Bennett, Jr., *What Manner of Man: A Biography of Martin Luther King, Jr.* (Chicago, 1964), p. 66.

But although white segregationists and racial ideologists sometimes invoked Washington's name, and especially his Atlanta Address, in defense of their views,[3] when most Negroes used his name it was in an unfavorable sense. Kenneth B. Clark, the Negro psychologist, for example, declared that the Black Power movement, while disguised as racial militance, was in reality the contemporary form of Washingtonian accommodation. "While Booker T. made his adjustment to and acceptance of white racism under the guise of conservatism," said Clark, "many if not all the Black Power advocates are seeking to sell the same shoddy moral product disguised in the gaudy package of racial militance." The Atlanta *Constitution,* which had consistently supported Washington during his lifetime, applauded Clark's statement. "It will not please the strutting Negro militants to be branded quitters and accommodators of whitey in this era," said the *Constitution,* but it agreed that Clark had diagnosed them correctly. "They are the Booker T. Washingtons of this time who will settle for what they can get from the white man, instead of continuing the struggle for full rights."[4]

While Washington's name appeared to be either discredited or forgotten, some of his ideas retained a certain vitality and relevance. The urban crisis of the 1960's dramatically emphasized the poverty of Negroes and reinforced the Washingtonian view that the race problem was fundamentally an economic problem. It was frequently asserted that the salvation of Negroes lay in self-help. Negro leaders (and some white politicians) spoke increasingly of "black capitalism" and the necessity of encouraging the development of Negro-owned or Negro-operated businesses. Such programs as the Woodlawn Organization in Chicago, NEGRO (the National Economic Growth and Reconstruction Organization), and the Opportunities Industrial Center of the Reverend Leon H. Sullivan in Philadelphia, borrowed consciously or unconsciously from the Washingtonian ideology, and their promoters defended them in language in some ways reminiscent of the Tuskegeean.

The popular belief that Washington was little more than an "Uncle Tom" is not historically accurate. As recent scholars have shown, he

[3] See, for example, Rev. G. T. Gillespie, D.D., *A Christian View of Segregation* (Reprint of an Address made before the Synod of Mississippi of the Presbyterian Church in the United States, November 4, 1954, n.p., n.d.); Carleton Putnam, *Race and Reason* (Washington, D.C., 1961), pp. 90, 116.

[4] Atlanta *Constitution,* November 6, 1967, quoted in "Rap, Stokely and Booker T., a Document," *Journal of Negro History,* LII (October, 1967), 325-26.

was far more actively engaged in the fight against segregation and disfranchisement than most of his contemporaries suspected. But this champion of complete equality was the "secret" Washington, a person whom the "public" Washington went to elaborate lengths to conceal. The man whom the public knew was the conciliatory, compromising figure of the Atlanta Address and *Up From Slavery*. It was an image which Washington worked hard to build and maintain, and it appears that it will persist even though scholars have shown that it was only an image and not the whole man.

Bibliographical Note

The most important sources for the study of Washington are the Booker T. Washington Papers in the Manuscript Division of the Library of Congress. The Papers consist of some 1,000 boxes of manuscript materials, including Washington's personal correspondence, records of Tuskegee Institute, the National Negro Business League, the General Education Board, and other organizations in which Washington was interested. The voluminous correspondence with political figures, educators, industrialists, philanthropists, writers, journalists, Negro leaders, and rank-and-file Negroes gives detailed evidence of the varied aspects of Washington's career and reveals a much more complex man than the one shown in his published writings. The Papers also include photographs, pamphlets, and a vast collection of newspaper clippings mounted in scrapbooks which pertain to Washington and race relations. Information about the Papers is contained in *Booker T. Washington: A Register of His Papers in the Library of Congress* (Manuscript Division, Reference Department Library of Congress, Washington, 1958).

Negro newspapers—both those which were pro- and those which were anti-Washington—are indispensable for an understanding of Washington and his role. Among the most important were the New York *Age*, the Washington *Bee*, the Washington *Colored American*, the Boston *Guardian*, the Indianapolis *Freeman*, and the Cleveland *Gazette*. The files of most of these have been microfilmed and are available for purchase through the Photoduplication Service of the Library of Congress.

Washington's published writings are, of course, essential to a study of the man. Almost all that we know of his early life is derived from his autobiographies. Several books and a vast number of articles were published under his name. In some cases these were entirely ghost-written; in others they were written by Washington with the assistance of another writer. Nevertheless there is no reason to question that the ideas expressed were Washington's own. Among the persons who assisted Washington in his research and writing were Max Bennett Thrasher, T. Thomas

Fortune, S. Laing Williams, Robert E. Park, Emmett Scott, and Nathan Monroe Work.

Washington's earliest autobiographical effort was *The Story of My Life and Work* (Napierville, Ill., 1900). Much better known and better written was *Up From Slavery* (New York, 1901), which has gone through numerous editions and been translated into more than a dozen foreign languages. In 1911 he published another autobiographical work, *My Larger Education* (New York, 1911), which had appeared in serialized form in *World's Work* as "Chapters from My Experience." The first compilation of his speeches was *Black Belt Diamonds: Gems from the Speeches, Addresses, and Talks to Students of Booker T. Washington* (New York, 1898). *Character Building* (New York, 1902) is a collection of his Sunday evening talks to Tuskegee students. His more important public addresses are in *Selected Speeches of Booker T. Washington*, ed. E. Davidson Washington (New York, 1932).

Other books by Washington include: *The Future of the American Negro* (Boston, 1899); *Working with the Hands* (New York, 1904); *Tuskegee and Its People* (New York, 1905); *The Negro in Business* (Chicago, 1907); *Frederick Douglass* (Philadelphia and London, 1907); *The Negro in the South, His Economic Progress in Relation to His Moral and Religious Development* (Philadelphia, 1907); *The Story of the Negro*, 2 vols. (New York, 1909); *The Man Farthest Down: A Record of Observation and Study in Europe,* with the collaboration of Robert E. Park (New York, 1912).

The articles written by Washington are too numerous to list. The views expressed in many of them, and sometimes the articles themselves, were incorporated into his books. Some of the articles of his later years, notably, "Is the Negro Having a Fair Chance?" *Century,* LXXXV (November, 1912), 46–55 and "My View of Segregation Laws," *New Republic,* V (December 4, 1915), 113–15, should be mentioned because they are less accommodating in tone than his books.

The definitive biography of Washington remains to be written. *Booker T. Washington, Builder of a Civilization* (New York, 1916), by Emmett J. Scott and Lyman Beecher Stowe, was commissioned by Washington before his death. It is highly eulogistic but contains valuable information on some facets of his career. The first attempt at a scholarly biography was Basil

Mathews, *Booker T. Washington, Educator and Interracial Interpreter* (Cambridge, Mass., 1948). The book, by an author who was admittedly an enthusiastic admirer of the Tuskegeean, represents a substantial amount of research, including some use of manuscript materials now in the Library of Congress which were then at Tuskegee. A more balanced account, although it embodies less original research, is *Booker T. Washington and the Negro's Place in American Life* (Boston, 1955) by Samuel R. Spencer, Jr.

Numerous interpretative articles and essays dealing with Washington's role as race leader, some of them favorable, others antagonistic, have appeared. Among these are: Jack Abramowitz, "Crossroads of Negro Thought, 1890–1895," *Social Education,* XVIII (1954); Rebecca Chalmers Barton, "Up From Slavery," in *Witnesses for Freedom: Negro Americans in Autobiography* (New York, 1948); Horace M. Bond, "Negro Leadership Since Washington," *South Atlantic Quarterly,* XXIV (1925); Oliver C. Cox, "The Leadership of Booker T. Washington," *Social Forces,* XXX (1951); W. Edward Farrison, "Booker T. Washington: A Study in Educational Leadership," *South Atlantic Quarterly,* XLI (1942); Charles S. Johnson, "The Social Philosophy of Booker T. Washington," *Opportunity,* VI (1928); Guy B. Johnson, "Negro Racial Movements and Leadership in the United States," *American Journal of Sociology,* XLIII (1937); Gunnar Myrdal, "The Tuskegee Compromise," in *An American Dilemma* (New York, 1944); Herbert J. Storing, "The School of Slavery: A Reconsideration of Booker T. Washington," in *100 Years of Emancipation,* ed. Robert A. Goldwin (Chicago, 1963).

"A Critical Study of Booker T. Washington as a Speechmaker, with an analysis of Seven Selected Speeches" (unpublished Ph.D. thesis, University of Michigan, 1952) by Willis Norman Pitts, deals with Washington as an orator.

The research done by August Meier, especially his work in the Booker T. Washington Papers, has thrown new light on hitherto unknown or obscure aspects of Washington's career and character and on the Negro thought of the period. The following articles are significant: "Booker T. Washington and the Negro Press: With Special Reference to the *Colored American Magazine,*" *Journal of Negro History,* XXXVIII (1953); "Booker T.

Washington and the Rise of the NAACP," *The Crisis,* LXI (1954); "Toward a Reinterpretation of Booker T. Washington," *Journal of Southern History,* XXIII (1957). Meier's book, *Negro Thought in America, 1880–1915* (Ann Arbor, 1963) is valuable for facts and interpretation of Washington and his contemporaries. Louis R. Harlan, who is engaged in writing a biography of Washington and in editing some of his papers, has explored news facets of Washington's career in "Booker T. Washington and the White Man's Burden," *American Historical Review,* LXXI (1966). Charles Flint Kellogg, *NAACP. A History of the National Association for the Advancement of Colored People,* Vol. I: 1909–1920 (Baltimore, 1967), is a piece of painstaking research in manuscript materials which adds new details to our knowledge of Washington's relations with the NAACP and its leaders. The following articles by Emma Lou Thornbrough contain information on some of Washington's activities and his methods: "The Brownsville Episode and the Negro Vote," *Mississippi Valley Historical Review,* XLIV (1957); "More Light on Booker T. Washington and the New York *Age," Journal of Negro History,* LXIII (1958); "The National Afro-American League, 1887–1908," *Journal of Southern History,* XXVII (1961).

Du Bois' own account of his relations with Washington and his evaluation of the men are found in "Of Mr. Booker T. Washington and Others," in *The Souls of Black Folk: Essays and Sketches* (Chicago, 1903); and *Dusk of Dawn: An Essay Toward an Autobiography of a Race Concept* (New York, 1940). Two excellent biographical studies of Du Bois are: Francis L. Broderick, *W. E. B. Du Bois. Negro Leader in a Time of Crisis* (Stanford, California, 1959) and Elliott M. Rudwick, *W. E. B. Du Bois: A Study in Minority Group Leadership* (Philadelphia, 1960).

A brief account of Washington's most vehement Negro critic is found in "William Monroe Trotter, 1872–1943," by Charles W. Puttkammer and Ruth Worthy, in the *Journal of Negro History,* XLIII (1958).

The best general history of Negro Americans is John Hope Franklin, *From Slavery to Freedom: A History of American Negroes* rev. ed. (New York, 1967). The best single volume on the South during the age of Washington is C. Vann Woodward,

Origins of the New South, 1877–1913 (Baton Rouge, 1951). Valuable information on Tuskegee and some of the white philanthropists associated with the school is contained in Horace M. Bond, *Negro Education in Alabama: A Study in Cotton and Steel* (Washington, D.C., 1939). A recent study by Henry Allen Bullock, *A History of Negro Education in the South* (Cambridge, Mass., 1967), contains material on Tuskegee and on Washington's influence on Negro education.

Index

Abbott, Lyman, 8
Afro-American Council, 9
Age (N.Y. Negro paper), 15, 19
American Dilemma, An (Myrdal), 23
Anna T. Jeanes Fund, 8
Armstrong, Samuel C., 4
Atlanta Address (Washington, B. T.), 33–36, 83–84

Baldwin, William H., Jr., 8
Barnett, Ferdinand, 20
Barnett, Ida Wells, 20
  on Washington, 120–22
Barton, Rebecca Chalmers, 17
  on Washington, 150–55
Basset, John Spencer, 3
Bond, Horace M., 22
  on Washington, 132–35
Booker T. Washington, Builder of a Civilization (Scott and Stowe), 21
Bryce, James, on Washington, 106–8

Carnegie, Andrew, 7, 17
  on Washington, 89–90
Chestnutt, Charles W., 3, 20
  on Washington, 114–17
Civil Rights Act of 1875, 3
Civil Rights Cases of 1883, 3
Clansman, The (Dixon), 18
Compromise of 1877, 1
Cox, Oliver H., 24
Crisis, The (NAACP publication), 9
Curti, Merle, 22
  on Washington, 136–40

Depression (1930's), 22
Disfranchisement, 13, 24

Dixon, Thomas Jr., 2, 18
  on Washington, 99–102
Douglass, Frederick, 50–51
Du Bois, W. E. B., 9, 18–19, 20–21, 22
  on Washington, 122–28

Economic foundations of Negro rights, 43–49
Educational philosophy, 37–42

Farrison, W. Edward, 23
  on Washington, 144–46
Fortune, T. Thomas, 19
  on Washington, 111–14
Fourteenth Amendment, 3

General Education Board, 8
Godkin, E. L., 2
Gospel of Wealth, 1
Guardian (Boston newspaper), 9, 19

Hampton Institute, 4
Harlan, Louis R., 24–25
  on Washington, 167–73
Hayes, Rutherford B., 1
Howells, William Dean, 17
  on Washington, 90–94
Hughes, Langston, 17, 24
  on Washington, 160–61
Huntington, Collis P., 8

Jim Crow laws, 3
Johnson, Guy B., 22
  on Washington, 141–43
Jones, Thomas G., 8

Lodge Federal Elections Bill, 2
Lynching, 3, 72–77

183